Contents

Acknowledgements

I should like to thank all those who have read earlier drafts and have provided memories, suggestions, and encouragement:— Dorothy Barnes, John Brown, Jenny Dixon, John Dixon, Dennis Roberts, Margaret Roberts, and Betty Rosen. I have acknowledged in the text my debt to many of those teachers and lecturers who influenced my teaching.

Becoming

an
Eng **Long Loan**
Tea

Becoming an English Teacher is published by the National Association for the Teaching of English (NATE), the UK subject association for all aspects of the teaching of English from pre-school to university.

NATE
50, Broadfield Road
Sheffield S8 0XJ
Tel: 0114 255 5419
Fax: 0114 255 5296
email: natehq@btconnect.com

British Library Cataloguing in Publication Data. A catalogue record for this book is available from the British Library.

ISBN   0 901291 76 5

Cover design, typesetting and printing by Quorn Selective Repro, Queens Road, Loughborough, Leics.

Part 1

Beginning to Teach

Introduction

My purpose in writing this account of seventeen years of school teaching is not to explore my school experiences as a whole but specifically to recall and understand teaching as I experienced it. The sixties saw radical changes in the teaching of English. They were not random: we saw much that was wrong in the previous English curriculum and actively sought change. Through my membership of the London Association for the Teaching of English I both witnessed and played a part in the cutting edge of those changes. The sixties have since been represented as a time of uncontrolled self-indulgence, but I do not believe that what happened in English teaching fits that account. What we were looking for was an English curriculum that recognised and strengthened all young people's ability through language to think and feel responsibly about the world they were living in, and we believed that literature had a major part to play in this. Far from regarding this policy as an abandonment of values, we were seeking a way of teaching English that would realise democratic and critical values within the confines of an education system that was far from *laissez faire*.

The central theme of this book can be symbolised by some lessons that I experienced as a pupil during the early nineteen forties. When I thought about my secondary schooling I remembered a teacher of mathematics who invited us to discuss problems, usually in geometry. After giving us time to work alone, he would ask one pupil to come to the front of the class and to demonstrate his method on the blackboard, explaining his reasoning and inviting other members of the class to discuss it. (He was one of the few teachers in the school who did not have a degree; perhaps he had been trained for primary school teaching.) Faced with this requirement my contemporaries and I put diagrams and mathematical statements on the blackboard, all the while *talking through* the thinking that we had done. Then other members of the class asked for further explanations, considered our reasons for the adopting a strategy, and suggested other possibilities, at times moving into a general discussion while the teacher listened. Making our thinking public through discussion turned *the thinking itself* into the object of our attention. That is, the essential outcome of the talking was *reflection*, reflection upon the assumptions we were making, the cognitive strategies adopted, and the logical coherence of the argument. This can stand as a symbol of what this book is about, how I came to understand the central role of talking and writing in learning, not only in English, but in all subjects of the curriculum. It was this principle – the importance to learning of developing understanding and insight through reflecting aloud in collaboration with others – that underlies the concept of the classroom conversation that represents the culmination of my teaching of English in schools. It was also central to the research that I carried out later at the University of Leeds.

This book too is a demonstration of the power of reflection through writing, for the view of teaching which I have presented here did not pre-exist the writing. It was by writing that I not only retrieved memories from the past but, in trying to understand them, created new interpretive patterns that have enabled me to understand my experiences in a way I was not able to at the time. I can write only from the "I" I now am; the "me" of the fifties and sixties can only be partially reconstructed, an object not a subject. I had two purposes in writing this piece of autobiography, to represent how I was teaching English during the early and mid sixties, and to explore the influences, persons, theories and events that created the teacher I eventually became. Teaching is much more than skills, and learning to teach may require quite profound changes in the man or woman's ability to relate to young people, and can therefore offer a considerable challenge to the personality of a teacher. This book can be seen as relevant to the debate on how teachers learn to teach, but more importantly as a contribution to the cultural history of education during the fifties and early sixties. I hope that it will be of interest not only to English teachers but to all who are interested in the part played by talking and writing in learning, and in the processes by which teachers improve.

1 Preconceptions

My attempt to analyse the influences on my first weeks, months, years of teaching is hindered by my complete lack of any recollection of conflict or uncertainty at the level of general principle. There was plenty of hesitation when I planned lessons, but no sense of the guiding principles that *should* have been competing whenever I thought about my chosen career. Or was that too much to expect?

I can detect two influences which were not principles but perspectives that I was sometimes aware of. I can best associate them with my father on the one hand and on the other with F.R.Leavis who taught me at Cambridge. I have no recollection that I was ever aware that they might be in conflict, though they undoubtedly were. I shall describe each of these in turn, but first I must recollect my own schooling.

I must have taken some directions and preferences from my own experience of being taught. There was much that was good in my experience at Maidstone Grammar School. When I was about thirteen we had a master – to my amazement I have just remembered that his name was Edmonds – who was timetabled for Religious Education with us. In retrospect I wonder whether he was a non-believer, for he certainly made no attempt to teach us about Christianity or any other religion. Perhaps he had been drafted in only under the pressure of wartime shortages. Under his care we spent one lesson each week debating some current moral or social issue, and learnt how to manage our own discussions. It was so rewarding to us that four of us set up in the school a Junior Debating Society, organised it ourselves, and invited several members of staff to its meetings. From those meetings I acquired not only a taste for speaking to an audience but also a belief that discussion is worthwhile. I remember that one of the other boys made a habit of picking out a crucial term in any discussion and saying, "It depends on what you mean by ... ", a strategy learnt from Dr C.E.M.Joad of *The Brains Trust*. This is a valuable reminder that on the radio at that time the discussion programme of that name was presenting young people like me with a powerful model of how issues could be discussed analytically. The lessons in mathematics that I have already described showed me the value of bringing one's own thinking into the public arena. I enjoyed being asked to demonstrate and discuss my approach to a problem and found that it enabled me to reflect on my own thinking and that of others, in a way that contributed considerably to my grasp of the mathematics we were learning. I must admit that some members of the class who had difficulty on sorting out their line of reasoning found the experience of expounding at the blackboard an embarrassing one.

In later years at school I found the discussions in sixth form "general studies" exciting because they were intellectually challenging, but my negative experiences at the same age were even more persuasive. In sixth form history I was the sole student, and was being groomed for an Oxbridge scholarship. I greatly resented it that the history teacher, a very senior member of staff, sat me at the back of the room and lectured at me, showing no interest in me except as a sponge to soak up his ideas. In English too I was the only student, but Mr Lye who taught me English took a personal interest in me and my learning, sat down beside me to help me understand what was needed in sixth form essays, diagnosed what was wrong with my handwriting, and encouraged me to keep notebooks of poems and prose passages that appealed to me. I cannot claim that at the age of sixteen or seventeen I was able to utilise these experiences by telling myself that effective learning seldom takes place at arms' length from the learner's private concerns and anxieties. Yet a similar insight many years later was to shape my ideas about what I called "school" and "action" knowledge. Did these experiences of active participation in discussion as part of learning –and the lack of it – go some way to shape my future preferences as a teacher and educationist? I have no consciousness of having applied these experiences when I began to teach.

My father had originally taught general subjects in what was then called an Elementary School, but by the time we moved to Maidstone in 1934 he was teaching metalwork in a Central School – an elementary school with a few extra facilities – which later became a Secondary Modern School. I think it would not be unjust to him to say that teaching for him was a secure and well-paid job and not a great deal more. He did his work thoroughly, and was proud when his pupils' work was chosen for show in a national display of school metalwork organised by H.M. Inspectors, but I don't ever remember his expressing any sense of teaching as a vocation. He taught boys who came mainly from working class homes, some clever, some not. He did his best for them, and many of them were pleased to acknowledge him in later life, but he had few theories about their learning or what his lessons were offering them. He knew that some would use the skills he taught them in industry; others at home; others not at all. At the centre of my father's thinking about teaching was the idea of "good discipline" which was little more than seeing to it that boys obeyed him. He scorned teachers who "Couldn't control their classes". Once in the classroom, like other young teachers I was much concerned about "control", not realising the difference between authority based upon willing collaboration and that based upon compulsion and force. No one during my year of training mentioned this. Thus an over-simplistic view of classroom relationships had already been laid down as an underlying assumption when I began a preliminary "teaching practice" at my father's school before going to Cambridge to begin my degree. I suspect that I had taken in much of the sceptical and even disillusioned perspective of some male elementary school teachers, and certainly had no high-falutin aspirations. From those weeks of observation and a kind of teaching, I remember only a very successful lesson taught by a pretty young history teacher to a class I found unmanageable. I could see she had them eating out of her hand but I couldn't see how she did it – a not uncommon experience during school practice, I suspect.

Cambridge was different, so different that I will not find it easy to explain. I "read English" – that is, studied the works of English literature – under the guidance of Dr Leavis, who had already made himself a reputation for a fiercely puritanical view both of the moral importance of literature in the community and for his scorn of the less then high-minded behaviour of many public persons, including those who managed universities. For Leavis, the teaching of literature was a religious duty, though he did not couch it in theological terms, for his was an agnostic religion. I learnt from his books (such as *Culture and Environment)* as well as from his own mouth that ours is a corrupt society, in which motives of power and social status have taken the place of fine and sensitive living. He believed that literature provides the most available storehouse of the priorities and sensitivities that make up the culture so sadly lacking in most people's lives. Those of us who intended to become teachers – and many of his students did – held the future of our culture in their hands. Young people needed to be protected from the corruption about them, exemplified in cheap fiction as much as in newspapers that trivialised their lives and advertisements that tempted them into useless consumption. However, Leavis didn't reify the values that he wanted to substitute as if they lay inert in the works of literature: they became available only through strenuous engagement with them and openness to what they offered, so that it was only through teachers of English literature that most members of society could have access to what might one day save us all. A central task would be instructing our pupils in "how to read", a phrase that did not refer to the mechanics of decoding a written text but to the interpretations, feelings and evaluations which he and his collaborators in the quarterly review *Scrutiny* held to be appropriate to particular works of literature. If we developed in our pupils a sensitivity to the moral and interpersonal delicacies of literature it would become a sensitivity that would inform their lives.

In retrospect I can see how this rigorous literary athleticism brought to our attention the importance of the students' active engagement with the material being studied. His own teaching tended to be didactic, but when challenged he was willing to engage seriously with students. When his paper on Dickens' *Hard Times* was published in *Scrutiny* I had by chance just read the novel, and

I disagreed strongly with some aspects of his account of it, particularly his failure to criticise Dickens' dislike of trade unions and his reliance upon personal charity to alleviate the suffering of urban workers. I wrote a critical reply to Leavis' paper and handed it to him. (I still have my reply with Leavis' comments written in the margins.) He devoted the next seminar entirely to replying and did so in a way that was encouraging rather than damaging to me. It was a fine lesson in how to value your student's perspective even when you disagree, and I still feel grateful to him. In spite of such points of disagreement, for ten years I saw English literature in general through Leavis' eyes, and only afterwards did I began to look critically at his belief in the moral efficacy of the study of literature.

Such was the strength of Leavis' personality – and our naiveté – that few of us questioned this elitist doctrine. We never asked whether those lost souls who read popular newspapers and cheap novels might not at times show qualities in their lives that we who studied Eliot and James would never achieve. Leavis' view of society was not right wing: for him the very corruption of the culture that he saw about him demonstrated how we were all exploited by those who held wealth and power. Many of his most enthusiastic students were socialists of one kind or another: but Leavis was no Marxist for he believed that a shift of power into other hands would not make our society less corrupt. Many of my socialist contemporaries saw his cultural programme as a way of restoring to ordinary people the cultural wealth of which they had been deprived, and I accepted this view. Typical of this socialist interpretation of the Cambridge view of literature and life were the books later written by Raymond Williams, though I did not meet him until many years later. I believed that my task as an English teacher would be to make the riches of English literature widely available to my students. It seemed a properly lofty aim with which to embark on my career.

These are the principles for English teaching that I derived from Leavis' teaching, though I do not know whether he would have accepted this version of what he taught.

- Essential to good reading is a meticulous attention to "the word on the page", the precise texture and meaning of the language used.
- *Sensibility* – sensitivity to the word on the page and its ethical implications – can best be developed through critical collaboration and discussion.
- The purpose of teaching English is to develop young people's sensibilities in living by giving them access to fine literature and how to read it.
- Literature will provide the basis for preparing young people for the language uses they will need in adult life in a corrupt society, and the practising of skills needed in the adult world must yield precedence.
- There is an established corpus of good literature and a right way of interpreting it. (Leavis did not see this as "high culture" but the only culture worthy of the name.)

- Pupils have to be guided to the "right" interpretation by appropriate teaching. This was represented as giving them the power of discriminating the good from the bad.
- Children's own attempts at writing may have a part to play but it is not a central one. Their efforts are only to be justified as a means of allowing them access to high culture.

It was the first two of these that were most important to my later development as a teacher. I took it for granted that the kind of detailed discussion of works of prose and verse that I had experienced at Cambridge, both under Leavis' guidance and informally with my contemporaries, was the way to create a response to a work of literature. This collaborative view of reading was not a consciously held belief but an unquestioned absolute.

The campaign to convince the world of these truths, which Leavis' converts took on with almost religious fervour, carried with it two dangers; one was a temptation to righteous indignation that can be seen in some of his followers to this day. Second, all those who have access to the ultimate truth about the world must be liable to feel that others are inferior beings, and this often led to an arrogance that certainly affected me when I began teaching. I know that I offended some colleagues at my first school by my certainty that the Cambridge view of English teaching was the only acceptable one.

I can remember no sense of conflict between the two perspectives, that from my father and that from my university teacher. Somehow the high-minded moral purpose and the pragmatic view of teaching as a job to be done coexisted happily. In comparison with these two powerful perspectives the "training" in teaching English I received at the Cambridge Department of Education was useless. The specialist in English teaching, who apparently had great expertise as a rowing coach, had nothing whatsoever to give to aspiring English teachers. His lectures seemed nonsense to me then, and I have no reason to change my assessment now. Nor did he come to see me teach English during the term of "school practice", but asked the headmaster, a scientist, to decide whether my practice had been successful. The psychology lectures given by Dr Thouless were well-planned and interesting but I could not see how they might enlighten teaching, though they threw useful light on testing. (I found Denis Harding's book on social psychology much more to the point. I do not remember any details, but I wonder whether some general ideas from it could have survived in a vague form to influence my later interest in the effect of group discussion upon learning.) The history of education – taught by the academic historian who was head of the department – was breathtakingly irrelevant, though I lacked the courage to tell him so when he asked me whose lectures I felt to be the most irrelevant of all in the department. All in all, much of the year of *training* to be a teacher was a scandalous waste of time, though I know from my wife, who was trained at the London Institute of Education, that a good course can be very valuable to an intending teacher.

The Certificate of Education course at Cambridge required me to spend the middle term of the year teaching in a school as a student teacher, and I chose to teach at Gillingham Boys Grammar School since this would allow me to live at my home which was only a few miles away. I am amazed how little I remember from what must have been at least a dozen weeks' teaching, for all I could relate would be anecdotes that have no bearing on learning to teach. I was allowed to meet only younger pupils, and had no experience of examination classes. The Senior English Master was friendly but taught me little, and I found conversations with two younger English teachers more helpful in learning to manage a class. The music teacher, who thought it inappropriate for someone without a music qualification to teach the subject, made it impossible for me to take on any music teaching as I had intended, so that I have never taught music. I remember enjoying poetry lessons; I imagine that my experience at Cambridge will have made me involve the pupils in discussing the interpretation as a matter of course. I asked middle school pupils to write about their attitudes to poetry, and analysed and reported the results in an essay that was part of the assessed work for the course – my first piece of empirical research, taking the model for this from the essays of George Orwell. The essay was well received by my tutor. For any student of Leavis there could be no question whether literature should be at the centre of an English course.

In the summer of 1949 I found that I would not be called into the Forces but was free to take a post, though I did not find a permanent appointment until the following January. I believe I did some voluntary teaching at my father's school. Then I spent several weeks replacing a primary school teacher who had fallen ill. I knew nothing about eight year olds or what constituted their curriculum, and I don't remember being given any help with this. My attempts to teach them were totally inappropriate and ineffective, and I remember nothing except one child in the class whom I liked. If I was learning anything from these experiences I cannot identify it.

2 My First School

My father's ambition for me, which I accepted throughout my years at school and university, was that I should become a teacher in a grammar school. It now seems strange that my father, a lifelong socialist, should have accepted unquestioningly so crudely meritocratic a view of *success*, but during those years such values were seldom questioned. I accepted this goal, and applied only for posts in selective schools. In October or November I was appointed to Carlton Grammar School in Bradford, which had formerly been named Carlton Street Higher Grade School. The name hints at its history: it had been set up near the centre of Bradford at the end of the last century when the city was ahead of its time in offering secondary education to perhaps a third of its children. Now that comprehensive education is widespread it may be necessary to point out the implications of teaching in "grammar" schools. Since grammar schools were able to select their pupils it meant that all the pupils were literate and all had left primary education with a sense of success, since they had been selected. Most pupils would be keen to succeed. A large proportion came from comfortable homes where education was thought to be important, though some parents would not have had an understanding of the tacit values of education that professional parents could provide. Such a school provided a young teacher with a relatively comfortable introduction to teaching.

I found later that Carlton Grammar School's standing in people's eyes was probably lower than that of any other grammar school in the city, but for all that it wasn't a bad school. However, after I was appointed the school buildings caught fire and were destroyed, so that in January 1950 I began teaching without exercise or text books in a decayed building that had been vacated by Bradford Grammar School. It was not a helpful beginning. As with most beginning teachers, my most urgent task was finding out how to survive in front of a class of pupils, and like other beginners I failed to realise that competence in choosing and managing appropriate sequences of work were far more central to what we then called "discipline" than merely imposing my will on young people. I was an awkward and shy young man, unused to dealing with adolescent boys, and I think that this probably led me at first to adopt a distant manner with my pupils. I have often been criticised for failing to make eye-contact with those I talk with, and in those early months this must have been a severe disadvantage in managing a class. However, I found when I was required to write reports on the class for which I acted as *form master* that I had a great deal to say about each of them, so I had clearly attended closely to them. I do not think that I was ever again to have such a powerful sense of the individuality of a group of pupils, yet I am sure that they would not have suspected this. It was not until I had been a year or two at Carlton that my interest in my pupils began to show itself in any warmth of interaction with them. I found that I enjoyed the company of some classes, and even began to make jokes. I now know that some young teachers bring this warmth and openness to their relations with their pupils almost from their first moment in the classroom. For me it was a long, slow journey, but I can identify significant moments in this progress to maturity. In the summer of 1950 a colleague invited me to join him and a group of pupils on a month-long visit to a village in Hessen, and my enjoyment of the company of my pupils and the German boys and girls made a considerable difference to my attitude to teaching. I also took responsibility for the under-fourteen cricket team, and this too brought me on to closer terms with pupils, some of them members of the *form* for which I had daily responsibility. Once I had achieved some ease in relating to my classes, I was ready to learn more.

As I have indicated, when I began teaching in the school in Bradford I had a strong sense of having different purposes from the older colleagues who were teaching English. My experience at Cambridge had given me a sense of mission, but my awareness of difference (and, I fear, superiority) was not matched by any clear sense of how to carry out the mission. The English curriculum that I found now seems to me to have been without shape or principle. My colleagues prepared older pupils for the examinations but seemed unaware of the inadequacy of the assumptions about language and literature on which they were based. In the lower part of the school there seemed no clear purpose either, even for literature. I remember the trivial plays that soon after my arrival were bought for younger pupils to read: one that remains in my mind was a coy piece about an ogre who thought he was eating children but was really eating the beef that his cook prepared for him under the pretence of cooking children. It was entertaining, but no more: it had no literary merits nor was the language demanding. But I don't remember asking myself why the pupils were reading it.

My initial practices were probably typical of conventional English teaching of the early fifties. The English for each week consisted of five or six lessons of only about thirty-five minutes, far too short a time for extensive planning. The current practice was to give each lesson to a separate topic, poetry, stories, drama, writing , and language work; the possibility of interrelating them into a single activity never occurred to me at this time. Stories and essays were set

for "silent reading" but were also read "round the class",
to read aloud unprepared passages of text. This latter made
break off now and again in order to explain, or ask my stu
though it made for incompetent and boring reading. Whe
allocated parts to pupils, but the reading took place either with pup
at their desks or standing motionless in front of the class. At that time I had no
idea how to engage them in acting. My experience as a pupil at school and
university influenced my teaching more than anything I had read, but the
more experienced teachers around me probably provided the strongest influence at this stage. They pointed out to me what "language work" I should do,
and this was later guided by out of date textbooks that were provided by
other schools within a few weeks of the fire. These provided exercises in traditional clause analysis and parts of speech, and also manipulative activities
such as correcting common solecisms in usage: they also contained lists of
"essay topics". I do not remember many of them. There was a book for
younger pupils written by Stanley Glassey who taught at Bradford Grammar
School, and another used with fourth year pupils that had been written by
authors called Moon and McKay and which I think had been used during my
own schooling. Dorothy, my wife, pointed out to me recently that since an
inexperienced teacher lacks a repertoire of purposes and activities, a "course
book" is almost a necessity, to provide activities to fall back on when prepared
work fails. Unfortunately the quality of the activities available in the text
books of that period was very poor. I "marked" carefully all the written work
I received from pupils, pointing out solecisms in spelling, punctuation and
other forms of usage. At the end I added a mark out of twenty and a general
evaluative comment, which was generally brief. I don't remember whether I
responded to the content of what my pupils wrote: perhaps I did when I was
interested in it. I certainly had no general awareness at that time of the importance of replying to what they had written (as against evaluating it) and it was
some years before I realised that the quality of what was written might be
influenced by how it was likely to be received. Occasionally I read pupils' best
work aloud, but I fear that this was to illustrate the nature of the values that
were guiding my assessments, rather than to celebrate the achievement by
sharing it with the class. I remember very little of my teaching of writing
during those years, but Dorothy remembers that she 'borrowed' from me a
sentence that I had given to my pupils as a take off point for a piece of writing.
No doubt it was reverberant and perhaps a little *purple*, inviting a particular
mode of writing as well as proposing a subject. It is unfortunate that neither of
us can recollect the sentence, but at least the memory shows that I was beginning to think about managing the context in which pupils wrote. At times I
tried to teach writing by selecting from a batch of *essays* (as we called them)
issues of accuracy, style or arrangement of material for comment at the blackboard, though I had the sense to see to it that the sources of these remained
anonymous. However, I later came to the conclusion that this was fairly

effective way of teaching, since it didn't connect with the writers' needs at the critical moment of composition.

The most enlightened part of my early teaching was the reading of poetry, since I did know that I ought to read it aloud to the class, and engage them in discussing its meaning. I didn't waste time in pointing out figures of speech or verse forms – I had learnt the uselessness of this at Cambridge – though the text books that were issued to me suggested these activities. In other aspects of English, though, my practices were quite unacceptable in the light of the values and priorities that I learnt later in my teaching career, neither my "training" nor my experience of "school practice" having provided more enlightened models. With some more able pupils my obvious enthusiasm for poems and stories must have given me advantage that at times out weighed my awkwardness of manner and clumsiness in relating to my pupils. I don't think that my learning as this stage came in the form of conscious epiphanies, but from a gradually increasing awareness of my students and their interests. With at least one class – I remember particularly a third year class that I was responsible for as "form teacher" – I took to singing folk songs as a means of encouraging their interest in poetry. This arose from the fact that we were using Auden and Garrett's lively anthology *The Poet's Tongue* which contained folk songs that I knew. It so happened that at Cambridge I had made friends with two American academics, Seymour Betsky and his wife Sarah, who introduced me to the American folk songs collected by Lomax for the Library of Congress. I had not only learnt some of these but had borrowed Sharp's *Folk Songs of the Southern Appalachians* from a library. It is interesting to notice the impact of this apparently irrelevant interest upon my relationship with my pupils and thus upon my teaching. At a time when what is now called "country and western" music was unknown in England, American songs such as *The Streets of Loredo* and *Casey Jones* generated considerable enthusiasm amongst my pupils. It now seems a very daring device, which both derived from and contributed to the ease with which I related to my pupils. I was encouraged by my friend Alex Eaton who was teaching French to the same class and used to take his guitar into lessons to support the singing of French songs. Experience had given me confidence, and confidence enabled me to become more open and attentive to the signals given by my pupils. This poetry teaching must have been successful, for when I came Leeds in 1966 I met in a local secondary school a deputy headmaster who had been a boy in that very third form. He said that he still remembered those poetry lessons and that they had made him a lifelong poetry reader. I have seldom had so warming a testimonial. During the months that succeeded my failed marriage of 1952, I began to realise that I was actually enjoying some lessons, which showed up as bright lights in the grey depression that clouded parts of my life.

The two older English teachers at Carlton kept all the fifth year examination work in their own hands, but in 1953 I was given the opportunity to teach a sixth form. There were only four students studying English Literature for A level, but this gave me what I saw as my first opportunity to put the

Cambridge programme into effect. I do not remember teaching the set books; one was *Great Expectations* but the others have quite gone from my memory. Perhaps the excitement that I do remember came from lessons in *practical criticism*, as it used to be called. Dorothy, who was teaching English in a girls' grammar school nearby, offers me a clue by reminding me that it was then that I introduced her to *Reading and Discrimination*, the book that above all attempted to put Leavis' values into effect for sixth forms. In later sections I discuss some of the limitations of this approach to the teaching of practical criticism, but at that time – still heavily under the influence of the Cambridge perspective – I am sure that I found it highly rewarding to introduce my pupils to practical criticism in that form, and was delighted when one of them showed considerable promise. Three students eventually took the examination; two were successful enough to gain university places, one for English and the other for social sciences.

After a couple of years I was invited to become an assistant examiner for NUJMB – the northern universities examining board – for English Literature in the General School Certificate, which was sat by students at sixteen, and mainly used as a leaving qualification. I was horrified by what I found during my four years as examiner. Much of the literature read was of limited interest to the pupils and some was so trivial as not to merit study, particularly since only three works were to be read during the year. The questions and the marking rewarded mindless reproduction rather than critical thought, and at times I thought that the chief examiner's views about the significance of the works discussed was ill-informed and even sometimes totally wrong. My overall impression was that the examination was encouraging and rewarding an unhelpful and even misleading version of the reading of literature, and that at times it was most unjust to students who were thinking for themselves rather than reproducing what Frank Whitehead called "ficts" , that is, rehearsing the contents of story, poem or play as if they were facts to be learnt. It was this sense of minor outrage that in London some years later was to persuade me to stand up and speak in a public meeting and join a working party of teachers, a very significant event for my future life and teaching.

At Carlton School I taught a sixth form but no fifth form, so I was having no experience of preparing pupils for the leaving certificate, but this was only one of the incentives to leave the school. In January 1954 I moved to Dartford Grammar School, nominally in Kent, but in fact a London suburb. The school's approach to its task was far from liberal, though I liked my colleagues, many of whom were good teachers. However, parents and teachers alike were more concerned with examination results than with the more intangible characteristics of the education offered, and at first I was locked into a very conventional mode of teaching. The examination form wrote one essay and carried out one *précis* exercise each week, both being little more than practice for the examination. I *marked* them with meticulous attention to detail, and spent lesson time discussing what my pupils had written, particularly in *going through* the précis which I quite enjoyed, for it demanded considerable verbal ingenuity, and it was not until later that I began to understand what an unrealistic exercise it was. I was falling into a routine dominated by just those inert certainties that Leavis had challenged, but I don't think I was aware of it. Rather, I was just *doing the job* as defined by those about me. I became a competent classroom technician, though I am a little appalled when I remember the dull irrelevance of much of my teaching at Dartford. The school with its authoritarian values and focus upon examination results probably discouraged reflection on larger goals. If I was troubled sometimes in those early years by a sense of dissatisfaction that I was not carrying out Leavis' programme I had no idea what to do about it. Perhaps it was this that made me grasp at the new ideas from the London Association for the Teaching of English (LATE) when I eventually became a member.

I was ready for change. When I hear English teachers speaking with disdain and disapproval of the very popular course books written by one Ronald Ridout I know that they were not teaching in the early 1950s. At that time apart from the literary texts, the only books available were collections of essay topics and of exercises in traditional grammar and in the strangely artificial form of summary called *précis*. In *précis* exercises, students were given short prose passages of various kinds – some quite inappropriate for summarising – which were to be reduced to exactly one third in length. No criteria of relevance were given to guide the selection of one aspect rather than another; no imaginary audience or context was proposed which might help the student decide what was relevant and what not. Nothing more unlike the conditions in which real summarising takes place could be imagined. Like the *précis*, the essay form in the school certificate examinations constituted a genre in its own right. Typical of these were titles such as *Uncles* and *Bridges* which could only be approached by adopting a lightly humorous manner in the mode of Charles Lamb. Such triviality left many pupils with nothing to say so that they fell back upon empty formulae; both Dorothy and I remember trying to persuade our fifteen-year-old pupils not to begin essays with the words: "There are many kinds of ..." – uncles or bridges, etc. After I had taught for some years from such books I was glad to find alternatives: even the works of Ridout appeared enlightened and helpful when they first appeared.

3   LATE: New Perspectives and Challenges

By early 1955 Dorothy and I were married and living in a flat in Blackheath. It was she who persuaded me to accompany her to a meeting organised by the London Association for the Teaching of English. The London Universities Examinations Board had set a particularly unsuitable English Literature paper that year and LATE had organised a protest meeting. I cannot remember what was wrong with the London paper; it was the faults of the NUJMB papers which I had marked that spurred me to stand up during the meeting and to speak with some passion about what had appalled me in them. At the end of the meeting Dorothy and I added our names to the list of those teachers who were willing to join a working party to develop a new literature syllabus and examination. As a result, during the coming year and a half we attended evening meetings of the working party, which were held at London University Institute of Education. The group proved too large and split into two, and at some point I was invited to chair one of the two sub-groups and eventually to speak at the meeting at which the two groups reported our recommendations to LATE members.

Those were the overt events, but they do not explain what the subjective experience was. I think I must have been unknowingly dissatisfied with the routines of teaching that had captured me, because what LATE offered me was primarily the excitement of new ideas. At the simplest level this included ideas for lessons and for examination questions, but beneath those practicalities lay the glimmerings of a different set of principles. At first these was no obvious clash with the priorities I had learnt from Leavis; *response to literature* (as the phrase went) was still central to the purposes of English teaching. Joining in critical thinking about my work proved enjoyable in its own right; I had no sense that it might forward my career, as many years later it did. Indeed, until perhaps 1963 when I thought of the possibility of promotion it was always promotion to the head teacher of a school, and not into the academic world. Challenged by the ideas of people like Jimmy Britton, Nancy Martin, and Harold Rosen I found new sources of life; they became friends and encouraged me to think differently and to involve myself fully in LATE activities. I became a member of the LATE committee; Dorothy and I attended all the meetings and joined enthusiastically in discussion. Finding that my views were consulted and taken seriously by teachers and lecturers strongly influenced my view of myself as a teacher. For the first time I became reflective about how I was teaching, yet – it now seems – not reflective in a profoundly critical way.

I don't want to underestimate the influence that Dorothy had upon my teaching at this time, though its manifestations are not easy to specify. Her personality has always been more open and responsive than mine, and she had moreover benefited from excellent training at the London Institute of Education, where James Britton, though working for a publisher, was already a significant influence. She had been a successful teacher at her school in Bradford, though during our time in London she was coping with a much more illiberal school than mine. We certainly talked about the lessons we had taught, though my only clear recollection of direct use of her methods is in the *choral speaking* of poetry. During her training she had learnt that poetry should be read aloud, not merely studied on the page, and that all the class could act as a speaking choir for this purpose. This required careful orchestration, with the class divided into sub-choruses and some discussion of "effects" to be aimed for in various parts of the poem, suggestions for this being elicited from the class. I heard Dorothy's accounts of choral speaking in her lessons and imitated them, but in the field of drama I was too lacking in confidence to learn from her. When we were teaching in neighbouring schools in Bradford Dorothy told me about aspects of her teaching of drama: she believed that the way to study a play was to *produce* it, though not necessarily for an audience, but at that time I was not able to learn from her practice. During our years in London I cannot recollect any particular discussion of general ideas, though once we had become members of LATE we must have discussed at length what we had heard and learnt.

When I first met him in January 1955 James Britton was a senior lecturer in English in Education at the London Institute of Education, and not yet the international force for change that he later became. His thinking at that time was probably far less developed that it became a few years later, so in what I write here I may be borrowing some emphases that became much clearer at a later date. Jimmy was already highly critical of the idea that English teachers should be *handing on the tradition*, emphasising in contrast the need to involve the pupils themselves in the processes of developing a response to the poems, stories and plays they read. Indeed, plays were to be acted rather than read. This emphasis on the reader's response did not at that time seem to me to be in conflict with the Cambridge values, though its emphases fell rather differently. We were to take more care of the context in which pupils were asked to write and we were to help them to be aware of a possible audience for their writing; preliminary discussion was essential, to help pupils see what kinds of things might be included and to enact a potential audience that they might address. There were to be no more *Uncles* or *Bridges* set as topics for pupils' writing; trivial middlebrow journalism was no longer to be the norm. In the mid fifties Jimmy was not yet firmly rejecting the teaching of grammar, but insisted that it should be taught in context and in a manner designed to influence the pupils' writing, rather than as a study in its own right. Indeed he had published a little book for use with eleven-year-olds, *English on the Anvil*, which illustrated his views on the teaching of grammar.

What do I remember from those LATE meetings of the mid-fifties? I know that I found Jimmy's lectures very exciting for the challenging new principles he put forward. Strangely, what I remember of them are the examples of children's talk that he introduced, many of them from his own daughters when they were younger. Without knowing it I was learning about the importance of attending sensitively to the details of children's speech and the intellectual and social functions it was performing for them. What remains in memory of LATE meetings in general is more pragmatic, though not necessarily directed to the classroom. In 1955 there was the conference on teaching literature held in a neoclassical house called The Holme in Regents Park, from which I remember not only my first public lecture (which I shall write about below) but also a discussion led by Barbara Hardy, then of Birkbeck College, of a poem by Empson. Jimmy Britton provided a powerful practical demonstration by sitting down all the teachers present and requiring us to write for twenty minutes without any preparation on one of a list of typical examination essay topics. In fact he stopped us after a few minutes, but I think that by then everyone present had learnt at first hand the unreasonableness of asking students to write *from cold* on such topics. As for the evening meetings that LATE organised, there was one at which Boris Ford led a discussion; I think he must have given us pieces of children's writing to evaluate but the occasion is confused in my mind with a similar evaluative discussion of reproductions of some contemporary paintings which he had organised some years before at Downing College. Nancy Martin spoke on the teaching of writing. A teacher called Gordon Taylor talked about lessons based on an imaginary village, in which pupils assumed roles and wrote *in role*. Derrick Sharp showed a demonstration lesson in which a class of eleven year olds approached a scene from Shakespeare by first improvising the incidents in their own terms. Not all of the topics were directly related to classroom practice, yet it is significant that most of these that I remember during those early years were of that kind. However, these minor changes of practice were unknowingly edging me towards a new perspective that in the long run would completely change how I taught.

A by-product of the LATE meetings was my first published piece of writing. In 1956 a group of LATE members was taken one evening to visit Woodberry Down, one of London's new comprehensive schools. While walking up one of the staircases I fell into conversation with Frank Whitehead, then a lecturer at the London Institute of Education, whom I had got to know during the meetings of the working parties on the examining of literature. I told him that when I was about eleven years old my imagination was dominated by the stories of W.E.Johns, and I expressed my concern at the continuing popularity of his stories with some of my pupils. Perhaps I also said something about why I found the values of the books potentially harmful. Frank was a friend of Boris Ford who was then editing and trying to breathe new life into the rather stiff and old-fashioned *Journal of Education,* and knowing that Boris was running a series on popular children's authors suggested that I should be asked to contribute. It is rather undignified to have to admit that my first publication was a critical account of the *Biggles* books. My prime concern in that essay was to show that many of the values enacted by the characters in those popular children's stories were undesirable in one way or another, for I had well learnt the Cambridge principle that through literature we internalise values, good or bad. My first draft was richly edited in red by the editor, Boris Ford, and in green by his assistant, and I might have given up in disgust had not Dorothy come to my aid. Nevertheless, once the piece appeared in print I felt much more confident that I had something to say to other teachers.

Already my new ideas were heavily dependent on Jimmy Britton. My twenty-minute lecture at The Holme was concerned with a method of testing pupils' ability to read *unseen* poems, that is, poems that had not previously been studied in class. Cambridge critics, especially I.A. Richards, had for some years emphasised the importance of testing whether readers could construct a *response* for themselves, rather than merely reproducing what they had been taught. In the school leaving certificate this led to the testing of candidates' ability to write about *unseen* poems or prose passages. My twenty-minute talk was an exposition of ideas that had been developed for the working party on the literature exam, and was illustrated by a set of questions which I had devised. My central message came from Jimmy Britton, though the examples I used were my own. The principle I enunciated was that a test of the ability to read an unseen piece should not leave the boy or girl to make their way unaided into the complexities of an unfamiliar work of literature, but instead should provide a series of questions which would *lead* him or her towards the essential meaning, imitating the sequence of questions that a teacher might ask to help a class. First the questions would direct the candidate's attention to necessary preliminary issues, and then move gradually towards major questions about the poem or passage as a whole. (I'm not now sure that is the right sequence for reading though it may be for writing about a poem, for I noticed that readers often *begin* with general impressions before looking closely at the details that might substantiate them.) Thirty years later John Seed and I carried out an analysis of the questions in a sample of GCE and CSE examinations, and found that the CSE gave more support of this kind, GCE questions still being more likely to leave the candidate to his or her own devices. My lecture seems to have been an early manifestation of what was to be a nationwide change of emphasis. I wonder whether Jimmy Britton's influence was important in this, or whether he and I were no more than part of a general tendency to make examination requirements more explicit to candidates.

In the mid-fifties I was ready for different perspectives on teaching, though at that time I would have been unable to formulate in general terms what

LATE "stood for". In retrospect I can see that at the centre of LATE thinking lay respect for the pupil, and his or her experience and needs. The teacher was to enlist the learners' interest and collaboration and avoid confrontation, a policy perhaps easier to practise in grammar schools than elsewhere. Rather than focusing upon the pupils' ignorance and lack of competence, the teacher was to develop their uses of language through engaging them in reading, talking and writing on topics that the students themselves would recognise as important. They were to practise writing in a realistic fashion for interested readers, in contrast to artificial exercises that no-one was interested in. Writing should be *for real* not *dummy runs*, in Jimmy Britton's formulation. The hope was that the students like adult writers would use language to explore experience and to construct symbolic equivalents for what they had not experienced, and that this would not only improve their control over written language but would contribute to their understanding of the world and of themselves. I believe that this was the policy gradually taking shape, though I may be making the formulation too explicit by anticipating the clearer directions that LATE achieved in the sixties.

During my last few months at Carlton School in Bradford, a new head-master, himself young and ambitious, had said to me that since drama was part of the English curriculum I would have to take an interest in play produc-tion if I wanted eventually to become a head of department. At that time it would not have occurred to me that his unthinking equation of drama with production ignored improvisation. Dorothy, who had been an active member of the Bradford Civic Theatre Group, also encouraged me, so I helped one of my Dartford colleagues to produce *She Stoops to Conquer* with pupils. Such productions were important since many head teachers regarded the school play as a major occasion for displaying the school's achievements, and thought that such productions were the responsibility of the English depart-ment. I fear that my treatment of plays in the classroom became no more enlightened as a result. I went on to produce *Androcles and the Lion* with younger pupils. It was a frightening undertaking for me as I had no experience of acting or production, and had never taken much interest in drama in performance, so I felt both ignorant and incompetent. Dorothy encouraged me to undertake the production, and gave me much practical advice about how to plan and carry it out. I cannot claim a brilliant success, but at least the production was trouble free, and gave me the confidence to undertake a production of *Twelfth Night* the following year, also with younger pupils.

More important to the slow progress of change was my participation in the LATE working party on the examining of English Literature. By chance the discussions of ways of testing literature led to the idea that there should be wider reading of novels and that close analysis should be confined to a few short stories of some substance. We failed to find an existing collection that was suitable for this purpose and the group spent a few minutes suggesting titles of short stories that might be included. A quiet member of the working party turned out to be an editor from Harraps, the educational publisher, and he offered to publish a volume of short stories if we could put an interesting one together. Reg Egford, the chair of the other working party, and I were asked make a selection and to edit it; the collection was published in 1958 as *Twentieth Century Short Stories*. It would have been inconceivable to me then that the book would still be in print and set for examinations forty years later. In 1955, however, it was the plans for an alternative paper that were at the centre of our attention, and the reunited working party eventually presented to an LATE meeting the joint results of our discussion, a distinctly revolutionary pattern for an examination paper. Some years later an examination based on our suggestions actually came into being, because Reg Egford was able to produce our draft at a meeting of an examinations board which had at last acknowledged that radical changes were needed.

During the two and a half years at Dartford I had begun to try out new ideas in lessons. They were not revolutionary nor did they affect my work with examination classes. I tried Gordon Taylor's scheme of making the writing done by a class of thirteen year olds more realistic by situating it in an imaginary village, in which each pupil assumed a role and wrote accordingly. I gave another class time to write at length (a *project* in the jargon of the time) on a topic of their own choosing, extracting information and pictures from encyclopaedias, books and magazines. The result was very mixed; probably success depended upon parents' ability and willingness to give their support. I don't think that at this time I could claim radical changes in my view of myself as a teacher. I would have said that I was, "Trying out some new ideas," though I now know that is often the first step towards more profound changes of values and the consequent exploration of other practices that they entail. Discussions in LATE were helping us to become critical of practices that we had previously taken for granted. Perhaps at that stage we were less ready to change ourselves than to try to change examinations and textbooks, since we saw these as part of the institutional framework that inhibited change. Members of LATE met to change the examination; this led to changes in how students were to be tested, and then later to the production of new teaching materials (the book of short stories) and to discussion of teaching methods. It was not until much later, however, that we took the next logical step of looking critically at our assumptions about how pupils take part in the learning. We discussed the roles open to English teachers but I imagine we did so less critically than we discussed examinations, for example. It was very important to us at that time to know that we were members of a radical group, willing both to criticise and undertake action (as with the working party on examinations in literature). But the critical discussion was not always very profound. I encouraged my pupils to talk about the poems and stories they read, but though I believed that eliciting my pupils' existing understanding and attitudes was an essential part of effective teaching, I doubt whether I could have explained why this contributes to learning or why awareness of pupils' perspectives is central to a teacher's role.

At the Dartford school I had not been given any sixth form teaching, so I felt I had to move to obtain more experience. After several unsuccessful attempts – my ability to present myself effectively in interviews has always been very limited – in the summer of 1956 I was appointed Senior English Master at a tiny grammar school for boys at Ruabon in North Wales. Dorothy at first taught part time in a technical college in Wrexham, and then took the corresponding post to mine in the girls' grammar school next door, until our daughter was born. Ruabon Boys was not a good school – in various ways and for various reasons, none of which need concern us – though many of the pupils were very able. It was hard to lose LATE but at least I had my own department, which meant that I had more opportunity to shape my teaching as I wished, though the poverty of the school's resources brought its own sharp constraints. My teaching of writing was certainly improved by my taking more account of the pupils' perspectives and helping them to move into a topic. For example, it was there that for the first time I tried working with a class to construct a set of notes for a piece of writing, helping them to find some order in the ideas that they were able to propose, by writing what they suggested on the blackboard. This arose from a conversation after a LATE meeting: LATE, though at a distance, was standing me in good stead.

Even when I was teaching at Dartford, Dorothy and I were taking the teachers' journal *Use of English,* which has always spoken for the Cambridge view of English teaching. It is difficult to assess how much this influenced our teaching at that time; I have looked through the volumes from those years, finding no particular paper that had influenced my teaching, but reading the journal must have reinforced the perspective that I had taken from Leavis and his collaborators. During our years at Ruabon I began to receive books to review, some being children's literature but others more theoretical. One was an introductory work on linguistics, which gave me my first taste of an area of study that was later to interest me greatly and influence my work as a university lecturer. It is difficult to assess the effect on teaching of the other kinds of apparently unconnected learning that a teacher engages in during free time.

My teaching of poetry certainly changed at Ruabon, but it was hardly a principled change, even though I claimed that by helping younger pupils to attend to the detailed texture of works of literature, especially poetry, it was possible to improve their writing. This was more the result of the physical conditions under which I was working than of Leavis' emphasis upon "the words on the page". At Ruabon School the grant for English books was so small that after I had bought the necessary books set for examinations, I had money only for two new sets of books to be distributed amongst eight classes. I decided to spend the money on novels and plays, so that in order to read poetry with our pupils my colleague and I were forced to have them copy poems we had written on the blackboard, and this laborious necessity meant that I tended to choose short poems that invited close study. At this stage, unfortunately, it did not occur to me that I could just read poems to my pupils, since I assumed that close study was essential. Thus the kind of attention to texts that I had learnt to value at Cambridge remained unchallenged. I still have the notebook into which I copied poems that I was going to use with a class, and they throw interesting light on my reading at the time. Amongst them are several poems by the contemporary Welsh poet, R.S. Thomas. Dorothy and I had attended a local lecture on contemporary poetry by Professor John Danby, and he had recommended the poems of Thomas, which I had borrowed from a library and liked. There are also, for example, poems by Sidney, Emily Dickinson, Frost, Edward Thomas, Cowper, Clare, Pound and Eliot (*Prelude* and some lines from *Prufrock*), many of them unusual enough to show that I was choosing the poems myself, not using an anthology. The presence too of Thomas Hardy's poem *The Man He Killed* and a poem by John Wain about the atomic bomb suggests that I was already willing to set up discussion of current social and political issues with my classes. At this time, my teaching was still being more directly influenced by my reading of novels and poetry than by books or articles about teaching.

My confidence was clearly increasing since I felt able to use this poetry teaching as a basis for advice to others in an article written in 1957 or 1958 for *Use of English*. This article, 'Reading and Writing in the First Form', throws considerable light on my teaching at this time, and on the values that underlay it. I first explained the purpose of the work in terms I certainly would no longer use.

> If [pupils] are offered poetry that is physically alive, they can learn to respond for themselves to richness of verbal texture. Even eleven year olds can pick out the strikingly forceful phrase, can learn that rhythm is not a matter of regular thumps, and can discuss the difference between the poet's chosen word and a non-committal pseudo-synonym.

The emphasis on the surface characteristics of literary texts is typical of a Cambridge approach. Although "physically alive" was not a phrase that Leavis would have used, "verbal texture" was. What these phrases meant to me can be seen from examples of lessons that I described in the article. For one lesson with the class of eleven-year-olds I devised two short narrative passages, one concerned with lively and enthusiastic action and the other with slow unemphatic movement. Both I wrote on the blackboard using only non-committal verbs, and asked the form to copy the passages, supplying their own verbs. Then we took each verb separately and discussed their suggestions, not to choose the best but to distinguish between them. This was followed in a later lesson by examining from a similar perspective the verbs in passages of action taken from adventure stories. This focus upon surface characteristics led to a concern with the mechanics of composition which contrasts sharply with the emphasis on meaning and intent – upon the recording of first-hand experience – that was to characterise my later teaching.

Lesson time – I don't know how much – was given to the writing of poetry. Because Ruabon School was so short of textbooks and technical support – there were no duplicating machines, for example – I was forced to make a great deal of use of the blackboard. By now I was taking the view that written work needed to be *prepared* in preceding lessons, a far cry from the older School Certificate essay which seemed to make the assumption that a competent writer could write on any subject at the drop of a hat. (Perhaps Jimmy Britton's demonstration at The Holme was bearing fruit.) At Ruabon I was not yet concerned about creating a realistic purpose and audience, but – perhaps without realising it – was letting the pupils know what kind of style I wanted. It must have been during the years at Dartford or at Ruabon that I came across *Education and the Poetic Spirit* by Marjorie Hourd, and tried out the methods she suggested for helping pupils to write. The class were invited to close their eyes and all imagine some object: her example was a large spider on the classroom wall. They were then to think of phrases that characterised it, and jot them down. Next many of the phrases were written on the blackboard. I cannot remember whether we went on to work further at the stock of quasi-poetic material that resulted, or whether it was left as a resource for the class to use as they began to write. At other times after asking my pupils to jot down phrases related to a suitable topic, I went to the blackboard and asked for suggestions for an opening line. Having written that down I asked for further phrases. Some of those suggested were postponed, some probably rejected, and others modified as I added them to the growing verses. No doubt the boys quickly learnt what kinds of language would be acceptable. The resulting verse was not impressive, of course, but the procedure did communicate an attitude to poetry writing and a frame of mind in which to approach it. (Some of the boys may have written verse at a primary school, but perhaps not, for I found them very inhibited when they arrived in the school.) Of course, this sharply defined a mode of writing, but in those days poetic writing was taken to be what we were aiming at. It was not until later that closeness to experience became important: Marjorie Hoard's approach led to the skilful construction of artefacts from a stock of commonplace, not the exploration of individual experience. In my teaching at that time verse and prose were treated as products of skill, rather than outpourings of felt experience.

My declared purpose in the reading and writing of poetry was apparently "to show the pupils that emotive language can imply an attitude". I don't think that I necessarily achieved that goal. Geraint wrote about a waterfall:

> A shining arc curves majestically
> Thundering down on the glittering rocks below;
> Little fountains rise from the commotion
> As if, trying to escape the tumultuous water,
> They take the air.
> Droplets of water dance like may-flies
> In the shimmering world.
> A salmon leaps from the tumult,
> And for one brief moment
> Hangs stark in the sky.

But Geraint was exceptionally able. Arthur's lines were more typical of what the class made of the lesson:

> One wet day as the rain slashed against the ship
> And made the deck squelch as it came down...

A message of sorts had been received: the verse exemplifies the language of observation rather than feeling. What the lessons appear to have done was to focus the boys' attention on the verbs and to let them know that a quasi-poetic inventiveness would be rewarded. It was a more restricted kind of learning than had been intended, but my boldness in writing a paper for *Use of English* shows that I was pleased at the result. Such an attempt to teach some of the skills of writing directly – in this case making pupils conscious of the implications of choosing one word rather than another – belonged more to earlier styles of teaching than to those beginning to become common: four years later I would not have been engaged in the teaching of writing skills out of context. I can now see that the earlier approach had some virtues.

During the mid-fifties a new idea appeared in the discussions of LATE. If we were trying to convey to our students that writing about our experience in a range of verse and prose forms is a normal way of representing and reshaping experience, should we not be writing when we ask our classes to do so? I seem to have taken this seriously since in my notebooks from 1954 onwards appear various pieces of verse that I wrote during lessons with pupils of various ages. In each case I had attempted the same topic as I had assigned. Several of the pieces are *haiku*, in imitation of the very compressed Japanese verse form, which depends on the sharp collocation of images within the seventeen syllables allowed. This was a practice that I continued when I moved to my next school. I remember that with one class I collected all the *haiku* that my pupils had written, had them duplicated as a booklet, and made it available around the school. It was an attempt to see to it that the writing gained validity through having a wider audience than one teacher.

In one lesson with a class of eleven year olds I turned their attention towards an urban milieu, not far away even in rural North Wales, for many of the boys came from mining villages. In preparation for writing I asked my pupils to suggest what would be in a film set of a slum street and I wrote their answers on the blackboard. No doubt the items suggested came more from the films they had seen than from their own lives. Then I asked for suggestions of detached phrases that could be used to describe what would be included in the set, and wrote many of them on the blackboard. They were not just listed but organised into a pattern, with the aid of clusters, and linking lines, arrows and equivalences. I was trying to show my pupils something of my own procedures when organising my thoughts before writing. Nearly half of the suggested phrases I omitted, apparently regarding such censorship as a valuable teaching device, an oblique way of lending some of my values in selecting or rejecting phrases without imposing adult conventions too strictly. I can now see that the silent ignoring of suggestions might have been quite damaging to some pupils, though at that time I was in no doubt that it was my task to hand over my linguistic perceptions and values. It now seems very significant that I was encouraging my pupils to reflect, to make their thinking the object of thought, and also that I was using graphic symbols as well as words as a medium for organising thought. That was a considerable advance for a teacher brought up upon literature. When it came to the writing I expected them not to use what was on the blackboard but to go through a similar process for themselves. These sentences are probably representative of what my eleven year olds wrote on the topic *A Slum Street*:

> "When the dustcart arrives it makes a clatter on the battered roads,
> and makes the cats scramble down the street and through the fence
> into the gasworks. The sky is dark with smoke from factories."

Nowadays I have mixed feelings about this kind of writing , though it was a considerable improvement on the tame and mechanical pieces that they had presented me with on first coming to the school. In the article I quoted at length from the poems and prose pieces written by the class, and I am impressed by the fact that I was confident that this work would be of interest to other teachers. My then conception of good writing now seems restricted, since it was solely based on poetic models, so that writing that I was encouraging was highly poetic in intention; it seems not to have occurred to me that there were other kinds of writing that are of value. I put this blinkered view down to the influence of Cambridge, which was being reinforced by the *Use of English*.

Using the blackboard soon led me on beyond Marjorie Hoard's technique to new ways of interacting with pupils, not just to transmit my expectations but to draw them into joint construction of possible responses to the tasks, to give them a more active part in the making of meaning, a purpose that became more and more important as the years passed. With older pupils I used the blackboard not only for poetry but also for preparing for writing about more impersonal topics. The pupils would offer suggestions for what might be included in an *essay* and I would write these suggestions on the blackboard, trying to arrange them in a sequence and pattern that would help the class to find an order for their ideas when they wrote. The effort to synthesise ideas in a diagram not only enabled most of the class to join in the construction of ideas but helped them to see for themselves what was possible and acceptable. At this stage I was probably mainly asking for more and more suggestions. The values we have since associated with "oracy" were still some distance away, for it was later, in the next school, that I saw the possibility of referring the material on the blackboard back to the pupils for further consideration and discussion, so that the talk became more of a collaboration. New ways of working by giving pupils a more active role were opening up, though it is hard so long afterwards to remember how far I was aware of it. I was certainly enjoying teaching more than ever before, and this was not merely the pleasure of developing skills but that I was more capable of warm relationships with pupils. The influence of LATE on my teaching still only appeared in an oblique manner: I'm not sure whether this is a mark of my insensitivity to LATE values, or evidence that the association had not yet moved to the values that were to characterise it later, especially belief in the importance of encouraging the students' to explore in writing their own ways of experiencing the world. LATE disapproved of using lessons to shape pupils' perceptions and language in a way dominated by the teacher's preconceptions, and was suspicious of *fine writing* for its own sake. However, I can see that the increased interaction with the pupils in preparation for writing was a valuable change that I owed at least in part to the influence of Jimmy Britton, Harold Rosen and Nancy Martin.

I think that it was during the years at Dartford that I first made my first uncertain steps towards creating a wider audience for my pupils' writing and this led almost accidentally to the first work in small groups. I had probably used *wall newspapers* even at Carlton, since I think I can remember being involved as a schoolboy in producing one, though it was done outside lesson time. Wall newspapers were imitation newsheets written by pupils and pinned to the walls of a classroom, usually dealing with matters only of interest to the pupils themselves. These were prepared by groups of pupils who organised their own writing, editing and presentation, using several lessons to do so. It was probably my first move towards giving my pupils more control over the content and pacing of their work. It did not feel to be a radical change but merely an interesting variation, designed to encourage pupils to write about topics that interested them. I believe that many other English teachers were doing the same. At that time we were more interested in it because it provided slightly more realistic occasions for writing rather than as an oblique way of beginning to study public media of communication. It was to be some years before the latter would influence our thinking, and even then the Cambridge distrust of the media would at first limit the work to destructive analysis.

It was clear that most of my sixth form students were in need of considerable help in learning how to interpret the works of literature they were studying for the Higher School Certificate examination. I still retain all the notes I made for sixth form teaching at Ruabon, including *Lear, Hamlet, Winter's Tale, Coriolanus, Much Ado About Nothing, The Tempest, Dr Faustus, Murder in the Cathedral, The Duchess of Malfi,* as well as a wide selection of poets and questions on novels; the thoroughness of the preparation demonstrates how seriously I took that part of my work. To save teaching time I was timetabled throughout my years at Ruabon to teach all sixth-formers studying English at the same time, whether they were in their first, second or third year in the sixth form. With such a diverse group it was important to help them to talk and write appropriately about poems, plays and novels, so that to increase their general critical awareness and ability to read attentively I decided to teach *practical criticism* through the book *Reading and Discrimination* which had been prepared by Leavis' friend and collaborator, Denys Thompson, as well as similar materials that were being published in broadsheet format by *Use of English*. This provided passages of prose and verse for comparison and evaluation and carried with it the tacit assumption that for each piece there was an acceptable reading and a value that could be established by a competent reader. It was not until later that I came to understand why this approach might be thought unacceptable. At that time I saw no fault in these assumptions, though I was later to be taken to task for them by Jimmy Britton. In order to help the students approach unfamiliar verse or prose I devised a set of questions that they might ask themselves. These included:

> Is it a traditionally 'poetic' subject or something unusual?
> Is it developed logically, point by point, or has it some other shape?
> Is it formal and self-conscious or ... colloquial?
> Is the diction (choice of words) .... simple or elaborate, homely or unusual ... ?
> Is the writer teaching you ... or asking you to share an experience?
> Is he inviting you to share his dream world?

(I note with interest that I did not include the direct question, "What appear to be the author's purposes in writing this?" though something similar was implicit in other questions, such as the last two listed above.)

This strategy was a failure: the set of questions turned out to be no more than another set of textual problems interposed between the students and the literary text proper. It was a useful opportunity to discover that there are strict limits to what a teacher can do to support students' learning.

A similar purpose led towards what I now see as the most innovative teaching that I achieved at Ruabon. I was very aware that if I asked my pupils to read several chapters of a novel such as Forster's *Passage to India* in preparation for a lesson they would miss most of the implications that make the novel what it is. Of course, I could have then explained these subtleties during the lesson afterwards, but I was by then experienced enough to know that being told after the event is a far weaker way of learning then finding out for oneself when guided by someone else's prompting. (Nowadays the fashionable term for this is *scaffolding*, in the sense that the teacher provides a scaffolding of ideas, questions and procedures within which the learner works. It is thought that the scaffolding provided by interaction with an adult will enable the learner to carry out processes that would not be possible without it, and that after one or two experiences the learner will have internalised the process, so that in future he or she can achieve it without adult support.) So each time I prescribed for homework the reading of chapters from the novel I accompanied this with a set of questions for the students to find answers to: these required them to consider the motives of the author as well as of characters, to consider the implications of key passages, to discuss the evaluation that we were to place upon persons and their actions, to predict what was going to happen later, and so on. For example, one week I asked the current sixth form group to read the first five chapters of *Passage to India* and to answer these questions.

1. What is your impression of Aziz and his friends in Chapter 2?
2. What is the importance of the meeting in the mosque?
3. (Page 31) Why were Mrs Moore and Ronny at cross purposes?
4. What is the point of the last two paragraphs of Chapter 4?
5. (Chapter 5) Collect the faults of the Anglo-Indians.
6. (Page 48) What are the tone and implications of the sentence: "Mr McBride ... nice"?
7. Summarise the arguments Ronny puts forward to defend his attitude to Indians.
8. What is Mrs Moore's reply?
9. Comment on the nature and purpose of the account of Aziz' marriage.
10. What is the point of the last episode in the chapter?

(The questions had to be written on the blackboard and copied by the students: I can remember hurrying to the room before lessons to write up the questions before the class arrived.) All these questions appear to be interpretative, except perhaps Nos. 5 and 7, some of them being quite demanding for the younger students in the group. Question 2, for example, requires the students to realise that Aziz begins his exchange with Mrs Moore expecting her to prove like the other British women he had met, and for Question 6 they need to recognise the implicit criticism of MacBride's wife in the previous sentence. The following week I set similar questions on the next section of the novel, so that this eventually provided a framework for our shared reading of the whole, and a basis for discussion of more general issues.

At the same time as noting down their answers to my questions, the students were to quote the evidence on which their interpretations were based. In the lessons, I asked the students to discuss each of the questions in turn, joining in the discussion, but pushing my own views only when it seemed necessary to discourage interpretations that seemed entirely wrong-headed. (Or am I deceiving myself? It's hard to know when so much has happened since.) After a question had been discussed each student wrote on a facing page his notes on any new ideas that he had not reached for himself, and at times I set up a discussion about which of the opinions expressed in the lesson were worth recording. I was delighted with the success of this, not only in the pupils' understanding of *Passage to India, Emma* or *Pride and Prejudice*, but their increasing confidence and skill in reading novels. I would now dearly love to recover what the students made of the questions and how they were discussed in the lessons. I believed then (and still do) that the questions and my participation in the discussion *modelled* for them how to read a novel. The case against such an approach is that it may implicitly rule out of court any alternative readings that may arise from the students' experience of life being very different from that of the teacher. The approach produced excellent examination results for the class, though my intention was not only to deepen their understanding of the novel in question but to affect the whole way they read literature, and perhaps it did have that effect. I know that my sixth form pupils and their parents were very appreciative of my teaching during those years. Even in retrospect I cannot believe that my approach was so oppressive as to hinder the students' development of their own responses to reading. (Below I contrast this approach with the much more "liberal" one that I later adopted.)

I spent a good deal of time with one very intelligent and likeable pupil, John Stretch, whom I prepared for Oxbridge scholarship examinations. This probably turned more upon what I had acquired at Cambridge than upon any more recent ideas. I remember in particular sharing with him what I had learnt from an excellent book on Shakespeare's verse style as it changed from play to play, at a time when we were also reading Elizabethan lyrical poetry together. (I think the book was *The Janus of Poets*, but although I still have the notes I made on it they do not include the title and author; the world of academia was very far away.) The two lines of understanding combined when John offered me an excellent pastiche of a sonnet by Sidney. He duly won an open scholarship to Oxford. Although this teaching in a "tutorial" mode was enjoyable and gave me a strong sense of success, I don't think it contributed to my understanding of class teaching. It would be good in ordinary lessons to share the intellectual excitement generated for both tutor and student in the course of such an intense one-to-one collaboration, but I have seldom achieved it with a class, and then only for a brief period, perhaps part of a lesson.

It is interesting to notice that the reading and writing of poetry was still central to all levels of my teaching. My two and a half years of membership of LATE had not challenged my assumption that literature should be central to English teaching, and I had been perfectly happy to learn from what I heard at meetings of the association. LATE and the "London approach to English teaching" have often been misrepresented through too simplistic a contrast with "the Cambridge approach". Cambridge has been associated with "literature" and London with "language", an absurd simplification, as any member of LATE in those days would know. During the fifties, literature was firmly central to the London tradition; Jimmy Britton was not alone in his delight in poetry. This chimed in with the belief that all children should be encouraged to deal with aspects of their own experience in writing poems, stories or semi-autobiographical pieces. In later years this focus upon pupils' first-hand experience forced us to recognise that much of the literature read in schools spoke with a different language and about different kinds of life from that of many pupils from working class families. When LATE began to consider the implications of these cultural differences, a gulf did begin to open between London's central concerns and those of Cambridge, but the division was never one of literature against language. For years I was perfectly comfortable to combine my Cambridge preconceptions with those of London until the occasion in 1959 or 1960 when James Britton challenged my sixth form teaching of *practical criticism*. At the time, that confrontation seemed more embarrassing than important: it is now in retrospect that it seems significant of a radical change that was taking place in our thinking about the reading of literature.

I cannot claim that my handling of drama in the classroom improved notably during the years at Ruabon, though I must have begun some tentative use of improvisation, since I can remember being concerned about noise during lessons in a room above the headmaster's study. At the public level, my success with the two plays at Dartford encouraged me at Ruabon to produce *Macbeth* with older pupils, in spite of some opposition from a colleague who had produced previous school plays. Other colleagues were willing to help, and their interest and that of pupils and their parents persuaded me to persist. The performances went as well as many school productions, I suppose, but even after three productions I did not enjoy the production or feel confident, and did not attempt another. It was not until some years later that I made a systematic effort to learn how to engage my pupils in acting in the classroom.

During my first year at Ruabon, Reg Egford and I were still editing the volume of short stories which had been one outcome of the LATE working party on the examining of literature, for *Twentieth Century Short Stories* was not published by Harraps until 1958. The introduction claims that the stories show "brevity and spareness of build" so that they "deserve to be looked at closely". Moreover, in D.H.Lawrence's words, they would "lead into new places the flow of our sympathetic consciousness". Cambridge was clearly not far away. Questions were provided on each story and these were not intended to test but to guide the reader's attention when reading. For example, on Lawrence's story *Odour of Chrysanthemums* the questions included:

> "What impression do the first paragraphs give you of the area where the story happened? Has this any connection with the kind of story it is?"
> "Say ... what the change was in Elizabeth's feelings for her husband after his death. Why was she ashamed? In what sense had she been

fighting a husband 'who did not exist'? What in fact is the story trying to show us? Is it the obvious 'You'd be sorry if he died'?"

The questions directed the readers' attention to crucial points in the story and persuaded them to consider what we thought were matters of interpretation essential to the meaning of the story. This example deserves detailed consideration. The first question asks for an "impression", not a description, and continues by requiring the student to make an interpretive leap to link the milieu with the events of the tale. The second question directs attention to a character's feelings by means of an apparently factual question, and goes on to ask for explanations that required interpretation and hypothesis. In the short question, "What *in fact* is the story trying to show us?" the italicised phrase does not ask for facts but indicates that the answer is *not* obvious in the text, and then asks for critical discussion of one possible response. ("You'd be sorry if he died.") These questions embody a view of how to read fiction that emphasises the need to be alert to implications and possibilities that are not spelt out in the tale. The reader's role is firmly an interpretive one, in spite of the introductory question about Elizabeth's feelings. This approach makes three significant assumptions: that the teacher has privileged access to the meaning of the work of literature, that it is for the pupils to find their way there under his (or her) guidance, and that there will be an exchange of views between teacher and taught. (I am not intending to imply any doubt that a qualified English teacher's experience of reading and discussing a wide range of texts should place him or her in a good position to help young people learn to read attentively and with sensitivity.) Questions like these seem to be addressed more to teachers than to readers, in spite of the assertion in the introduction. In effect they embody a view of what reading should be, and for present purposes it is perhaps more important that they also imply a view of how a group of students might work collaboratively with a teacher in building up a shared reading. These principles make an interesting link with my teaching of *Mansfield Park* at Ruabon and even with my earlier talk at The Holme.

After a couple of years at Ruabon I became restless for a different school and for access once again to LATE. I now feel some shame that I did not at this point move into a comprehensive school. It seems hard now to believe, but I did not aspire so high as the larger salaries these big schools were offering to the heads of departments such as English. It is far from certain, however, that I would have been given such an appointment without experience of teaching less able pupils. Nancy Martin of the London Institute of Education and LATE encouraged me to apply for the senior English post at Minchenden Grammar School in North London, and wrote in support of my application, so in summer 1959 I moved to London again.

5 Moving to Minchenden School

During the sixties when I was teaching at Minchenden, LATE came to mean something different to me from what it had before I moved to Wales. Not only had my experiences changed my attitudes to teaching and made me clearer about some of the issues involved, but (I now believe) the thinking of James Britton and the central group at the Institute had moved on and clarified itself. By 1959 I had been teaching for ten years, and I think that it was during the seven years at Minchenden that my most significant learning took place. What I learnt there about teaching – and some aspects of my pupils' learning that caught my attention – laid down a basis for my inquiries at Leeds into the talk of pupils and teachers during lessons and how it affects what is learnt.

For the first time I taught girls, for my previous schools had all been boys' schools, and for some months I found it difficult to adjust my teaching style. I think I had fallen into a style of banter that could switch quite quickly into the use of ironical quips to control as well as to entertain, and the intelligent and sophisticated girls at Minchenden showed me clearly that this was not acceptable. I think that in the long run the presence of girls made me a better teacher, more aware of the boys as well as the girls as people with unique experiences, and more open in allowing classes to see something of me as a person. This fitted well with the emphasis on *personal writing* that was becoming important, not only in LATE but from other sources, such as Alec Clegg from the West Riding. Looking back I can now see that this new emphasis was inimical to the teaching of skills that might contribute to writing, since it treated composition as a holistic process more dependent upon the writer's personality than upon learnt skills. This may be true of some sophisticated adult writers but its application to young people is more open to question.

To place where my teaching had reached in 1959, memory helpfully provides me with a snapshot of a lesson that I taught within a month or so of my arrival in the school. My new headmaster had mentioned that the HMI who was responsible for the school, a Mr Adams, was due to visit the school one day, but I failed to detect the hint. Walking along the corridor to a lesson with a second year class I chose the poem I would read with them, for at that time I did not plan every lesson the evening before as I later did. Mr Adams was waiting for me at the door, inquiring if I would mind if he sat in on the lesson. Clearly he took it to be his duty to look over the new head of department. As far as I can remember, I first read the poem aloud to the class, while they followed it in their books. (The poem was a short lyric; unfortunately I do not remember which poem it was.) I think I must have next managed to have some students read parts of the poem aloud, though what device I used for this I do not know, so that the poem had eventually been heard several times. (At Ruabon I was still sometimes using *choral reading* of poems but I think I had abandoned that by 1959.) Then I opened discussion about what the poet intended, incidentally checking their general understanding of its meaning. The poem must have overlapped into the pupils' experience for I remember that I managed to move them from the poem out into a lively discussion of related incidents in their lives, before returning to what the poet had to offer. In the course of this discussion I broke off to have them write a few sentences related to one stanza, and asked some of them to read aloud to the class what they had written. (A year or two later I would have included some group work, but not in 1959.) I ended the lesson by setting for homework some writing on a related topic, probably indicating that writing about some aspect of their lives would be not only acceptable but very appropriate. The headmaster told me that Mr Adams had been much impressed by the lesson he saw, and indeed it conformed to a pattern of varying the work within a lesson that was to become something of a cliché. A few years later he would have seen a very different lesson, but he never came again. It is worth noting that it was the poem that provided the context, the frame of reference for the different activities; at this stage the students' interests and concerns were only brought into a lesson if they were relevant to the poem.

Out of the blue comes another memory that I have not revisited for many years. It must have been in 1959 or 1960 when Harold Rosen brought a group of student teachers from the London Institute of Education to observe one of my lessons, and unfortunately chose to come at a time when I was teaching a class whom I was not on good terms with. At least, I recollect that I was on bad terms with the boys, and I can't remember the girls at all, which is strange, for generally I think that I was somewhat more aware of girls' attitudes and preferences than of boys'. I had chosen a poem for discussion, read it to the class and launched directly into an attempt to elicit their reactions as a lead into discussion. Boys and girls alike refused to play, and sat in silence whatever questions I asked. Harold tried to come to my rescue, as the situation was becoming embarrassing, and offered to lead the discussion in my place. Naturally I found this humiliating but I swallowed my pride and vacated the front of the class. Harold adopted a different strategy and instead of approaching the poem directly attempted to elicit from the class experiences relevant to those the poems was concerned with. His tone was warm and encouraging as he spoke to them, and it made me wonder whether I had

projected a chilly tone of impersonal literary criticism. However, the class, set
in a state of stubborn embarrassment, was not willing to perform for this
stranger either. I cannot remember what happened in the end; clearly it was
not a significant part of the incident, as far as I was concerned. What I did
draw from the experience was the principle that lay beneath Harold's inter-
vention, that the best way into a work of literature might often be to explore
whatever of the students' experiences that came close to the work's central
images or myths. I never made this a rigid practice; with many classes the right
poem laid out its own context, but it was added as a powerful addition to my
classroom repertoire. Previously, the poem or story had provided the framework for such lessons, with occasional sallies into first-hand experience; now
it had become possible for pupils' experiences to provide contexts for the
reading of literature. I had made another step away from Cambridge, but I
had not yet clarified whether the appreciation of literature was still the central
goal of English or whether it was no more than one means of helping pupils to
a wider understanding and competence in grappling with their lives.

One of my first moves upon taking over the department at Minchenden was
to eliminate traditional grammar from the syllabus. The LATE view was that
clause analysis and *parts of speech,* however they were taught, contributed
nothing to young people's control over written language, and that they added
little to their understanding of language in general because of the artificiality
of the traditional Latinate variety of grammar. I could see too that it did not
help greatly even with solecisms in usage, since those students who progressed
far enough to understand the complexities of a grammatical explanation were
precisely those least likely to commit solecisms. One of my more senior
colleagues was fiercely opposed to the elimination of grammar from the
curriculum, and engaged me in a sequence of energetic arguments before
school began each day. I came to expect to find him waiting for me every
morning outside my room. However, my younger colleagues supported the
stand against grammar and the change eventually took place. It was only
possible because a new examination removed the necessity of preparing pupils
for grammar questions. I adopted for the department a new "O" level paper
in English Language (which included an essay) that had been sponsored by
LATE during my absence in Wales, and accepted only grudgingly by the
London Examinations Board as a "special paper". The questions in this paper
had only moved a little way in the direction indicated by LATE principles, and
I had to fight continually to maintain even this small gain, in the face of the
examiners' clear wish to revert to their norms. Eventually H.M. Inspectors
published a report on "O" level examinations in English Language, and our
"special paper" was preferred above all others in England and Wales. Our
battle was won, and many other examination boards moved their Language
paper in the direction we had urged. Perhaps we did not realise how important this moment was in the gradual move towards a new version of English
teaching, for it was now patent for all to see that our pupils' ability to read
and write about a range of topics was more important than their ability to

carry out exercises in manipulating words and grammatical analyses. Moreover, the writing tasks and topics had become somewhat less artificial. It was important as a sign of further changes to come.

The changes, however, were not only educational, but were part of far wider cultural changes that were affecting attitudes outside schools. During the years at Ruabon I had continued to read literature but I had also begun to look at more theoretical books. William Walsh's *The Use of Imagination* impressed me greatly with its arguments for the importance of literature both in children's upbringing and in our understanding of children's development, but this did little more than reinforce the values I had learnt from Leavis. I found the arguments of Raymond Williams' *Culture and Society* very acceptable as a combination of Cambridge literary values with the priorities of socialism, but though I was ready to think about the relationship of schooling to its social context I had not reached the point of working out what implications this might have for my teaching as I did later with other members of LATE. Other kinds of literature were perhaps more important in changing our perspectives. These were the years of the "kitchen sink" novelists and dramatists, Wesker, Sillitoe, Bairstow, Storey and others. It was also the time of popular sociology and of quasi-sociological writing such as Hoggart's *The Uses of Literacy*. And LATE members were enthusiastic about Charles Parker's "Radio Ballads", radio programmes made up solely of snippets from people's speech. The reality and the value of working class life and culture was being pressed upon us, and with this a strong sense of its differences from what commonly informed the novels and plays read in schools. Many of us felt that school curricula presented a selective and mealy-mouthed version of life, which was not telling the truth. We were far from seeking the abandonment of values that are attributed to *the permissive sixties* but wanted to help our pupils to make sense of the real life about them, rather than a sanitised version of it.

What did LATE mean to me in the early sixties? At the centre it stood for less authoritarian approaches to teaching. At first this focused *for me but perhaps not for others* upon recognising the validity of children's responses to the stories and poems that we read together. No longer could I assume that it was my task to hand over to my pupils the right way of interpreting what we read. I had to accept that a poem would often speak quite differently to a twelve year old – or even to a sixteen year old – whose relevant experience of life would have been very different from mine. To assume that I already possessed the sole valid *right* interpretation would turn poetry lessons into mere preparation for examinations, and I had learnt – at Cambridge as well as at LATE – that poetry should change people's lives as a result of the reader's interactive struggle to make sense. Thus the pupils, their lives and their first hand responses to poems took on a new importance, though it was not until later that they moved to centre stage. (Perhaps this had already been explicit for some members of LATE; soon it became explicit for me.)

Although in the pages that follow I shall show changes in my teaching by describing some of the lessons that I taught and will occasionally indicate events and persons that were associated with particular changes, these will not be adequate to identify the dynamic that drove me to make changes in my work. Looking back I can identify five guiding principles that were important to the development of my teaching in the first year or two at Minchenden. From my first years as a teacher the ideal model of literature teaching that Leavis had provided made me dissatisfied with the teaching of literature that was implicit in many of the texts used in schools and in the way my first colleagues talked about teaching. Moreover, the messages about the nature of literature that were transmitted by examination questions and how they were marked were equally unacceptable. At the centre of this first dynamic for change was the sense that my pupils should be grappling with the significances of literature for themselves and not treating texts as bodies of knowledge to be "learnt". The second influence came from an increasing awareness of my students' responses to my teaching, and amounted to an acknowledgement of the potential validity of their experiences even when they had been unlike mine. At first I was perhaps over-sensitive to occasions when a class rejected what I had to offer to them; later I was driven by a wish to choose works that would relate powerfully to their sense of what mattered in their lives, partly because I had come to realise that tasks and topics that created boredom would be unlikely to develop pupils' uses of language or sensitivity to litera-ture. I was quite clear from the first that I did not wish to pander to current fashions: it was important to see to it that matters of real importance were addressed, and that the pupils engaged with them seriously enough to decide whether they could find them relevant. Indeed, during the sixties *relevance* became a key concept in English teachers' thinking, though it was never precisely defined. As I became more experienced this second principle devel-oped into something rather different as I came to believe that the topics that my pupils and I talked and wrote about should refer to the world as we were currently experiencing it. Thus the third principle was a conviction that the English curriculum should be related not just to pupils' private concerns but to social issues that were important at that time. I wanted to escape from the lingering traces of English for art's sake and move towards an English that would both support young people in their present lives and help prepare them for the future. Nevertheless, literature remained at the centre of my version of English, both by initiating topics and providing a frame of reference for them and by defining committed and personal ways of talking and writing about them. My fourth principle came from LATE. We were encouraged to place ourselves in the position of the students, and not ask them to carry out tasks that we would find uncomfortable. Later I took the principle further and did my best to make explicit to them the criteria by which their work would be judged, and this eventually led to my explaining to some classes of older students the purpose of the tasks I gave them. A fifth principle appeared as I became more and more convinced that teaching influences students' pictures of their roles and capacities as learners. Some teaching helps young people to feel that they are capable of choice and an active engagement with learning and other kinds of teaching encourage submission to the claims of authority, thereby encouraging passivity and making students feel inadequate. I began to see that teaching might have political implications; since I wanted to teach in a way that would prepare my pupils to participate in a critical democracy, this had powerful implications for how I worked with classes. This list of principles is in one sense misleading, since I could certainly not have made all of them explicit at that time, but I believe that they go some way towards identifying what drove me towards change during those years.

I must not underestimate the changes that had already taken place in my teaching during the years at Ruabon and that continued at Minchenden. With most of my classes I aimed to set up discussions that took off from some work of literature but moved out into areas of the pupils' experience before returning. Naturally classes varied in their willingness to join openly in talking about their private concerns. I remember a second year class that seemed different from the others in that the boys and girls were unusually willing to share their experiences and feelings, probably because they trusted one another. By twelve to thirteen years of age adolescence had usually overtaken my sophisticated London pupils; the boys and the girls in some classes, though highly aware, treated one another with cool distance tinged with suspicion, that sometimes erupted into conflict and dislike. But this group was different. The boys and girls liked one another; one could see them talking and playing together at *break* and lunch time, yet there seemed no flirtatiousness in their relationships. They were not immature: at times I was amazed at the maturity and openness of their talk during lessons. On one occasion we read a poem that mentioned some aspect of death. I don't remember what poem it was, and I was certainly not intending to set up a discussion about death. It was the class that set out to tell about their experiences; I would not have dared to ask them. Unfortunately I can recall only one anecdote: one boy spent his weekends caddying for golfers on a local golf course, and he told how not long before a golfer had died in front of him from a heart attack. The boy had clearly been deeply shaken by the experience but he was able to tell of the event and its effects on him quite calmly. The trust and confidence of these pupils in one another allowed them to talk openly about such experiences that would otherwise have been kept hidden. I invited the pupils to write about death for homework. The week-end caddie wrote about his experience and another wrote about visiting an elderly relative in hospital. One twelve year old boy – I think his name was Nigel – who was well known in the class to be an enthusiastic fisherman, wrote:

THE DEATH OF A PERCH

The weekend before last I was fishing down at Boxer's Lake with two of my friends, Paul and Boomer (Allan). It was under a Large Oak and I had just caught a small perch and rebaited. There was an obstruction on Boomer's line and he made a faulty cast, and he crossed my line. He brought it in a little way and tried to jump my line. His tackle tangled up round mine, but luckily it slid up my line to the bank. I could see that it would take about three minutes to undo the tangle. Just before the mess was undone, my line went slack; I struck about half a minute too late and I hooked the fish's guts. I got out my disgorger and hauled in the fish. It was a perch, about three inches bigger than the first. I picked it up carefully because of its sharp fins and gills, and its rough skin. I ran the disgorger down the line and made contact with the hook. I twisted, pushed and twisted again and then it came free. I reckon that half its throat must've come out. Blood was streaming out of its gills. I weighed it quickly and it registered 3½ oz. I put it back in the water and tried to revive it by moving it forwards through the water, but it died though it recovered slightly. I was sorry because it could have grown into a nice sized fish. One thing I noticed is that when the hook came free, it suddenly stiffened out; its fins and gills stuck out and its mouth opened and stuck out and stayed stiff for a while. So I think that a tale I've heard that fish haven't got nerves isn't true. If Boomer hadn't crossed me, it would never have happened.

I was more pleased with this piece than with others that showed more obvious skill with words, and the reason for this was that by this time I was valuing very highly any writing that appeared to engage with parts of my students' lives that were important to them. I wanted their writing to be very unlike traditional school exercises and to become instead attempts to reshape their interpretations of experience. This boy seemed to me to by trying to come to terms with an unfamiliar sense of guilt at aspects of his favourite pastime that he had not previously acknowledged. That was what *personal writing* ought to be used for, I thought, re-evaluating aspects of one's experience. (It occurs to me that it was Nigel who seemed to be central to the unusual social relationships of the class, but I do not know what significance that has.)

My sixth form teaching too changed radically: at an LATE meeting soon after our return to London I was taken to task severely by Jimmy Britton for talking with approval about teaching from Denys Thompson's book *Reading and Discrimination*. The pattern of teaching that was implicit in the book was one I had become familiar with as a pupil of Leavis at Cambridge, where it was sometimes called *practical criticism*. Students were usually presented with *unseen* passages for comparison and comment with the intention of teaching them to attend to the detailed texture of prose and verse, so they become able to *discriminate* (a crucial Cambridge term) and make comparative judgements of value. The poems or prose passages usually had something in common, perhaps the topic or the verse structure, but were contrasted in other ways. The students were invited to comment on the pieces, but there was an implicit expectation that one was to be approved and the other disapproved of. That is, the students were not to open themselves to what the verse or prose had to offer, but rather to sit in judgement. For those familiar with the values promulgated by *Scrutiny* it was often easy to predict which was to be approved; one exercise puts Donne's *Batter my heart, three person'd God* beside a hymn by Cowper. Another presents O'Shaughnessy's *We Are the Music Makers* for critical comment.

> We are the music makers
>   And we are the dreamers of dreams
> Wandering by lone sea-breakers,
>   And sitting by desolate streams;
> World-losers and world-forsakers
>   On whom the Pale moon gleams:
> Yet we are the movers and shakers
>   Of the world for ever, it seems.
>
> With wonderful deathless ditties
>   We build up the world's great cities … .

and so on. Students who have internalised the *Scrutiny* ground rules will know that they are not to discuss whether the claims being made for the influence of poets upon political events are excessive but to attend to the texture of the verse. The Tennysonian vowels and rhythms of the first four lines establish a drowsily intoxicated atmosphere, perhaps felt to be proper to poetry. Yet for all the poet's confidence the stanza ends with unintended bathos: *it seems* – brought in to complete the rhyme – throws a cloud of apparent doubt upon the main assertion about power, a doubt that can hardly have been intended by the poet. The competent critic will also point out that even over a hundred years ago the rhyming of *great cities* with *deathless ditties* would inevitably have had a comic affect. Indeed one wonders how any writer could miss the undignified implications of the word *ditties*. (In illustrating what was expected of the student I find myself slipping once again into the tone of coolly distant reproof felt to be appropriate in *Scrutiny*.) The teacher's task at the end was to point out those characteristics of the poems that made some to be approved and other to be rejected, with the intention of teaching students to "discriminate".

Work in "practical criticism" was held to create sensitive readers by making available to pupils the values by which right judgement was to be made, and this in turn was to contribute to ethical sensitivity in their lives. In retrospect I can see that in trying to move young readers into this arid and distinctly adult way of looking at literature we were not necessarily helping them as readers, whatever its relevance to examinations. The poems that were to be rejected often offered more to younger readers that the poems to be approved: mature sonnets by Donne take some growing into. It seems a poor way of encouraging an interest in poetry to reject those poems students like, even if they appear trivial or meretricious – a favourite *Scrutiny* word – from a mature perspective. The approach ignores the extent to which any reader is involved personally in the construction of a work of literature: there is not just one valid reading. Moreover, to short-circuit the process by which each reader develops an understanding of a complex work by imposing a ready-made interpretation may be to encourage the mechanical fulfilment of others' expectations.

At the LATE meeting I argued that by using the paired passages of prose or verse provided in the text it was possible to help older pupils to *discriminate*, to grasp the underlying values and principles that should inform our evaluation of the works. During the discussion that followed, Jimmy Britton made it abundantly clear that this evaluative approach to the sixth form teaching of literature was entirely unacceptable. In his view I should have been encouraging pupils to explore the significance of each poem or prose passage, but instead I was interposing a set of evaluative preconceptions that were external and potentially stultifying, which were in danger of devaluing the students' responses and with them their ability to make sense of stories and poems for themselves. At worst the approach would encourage artificiality and superciliousness. Jimmy did not actually say all this but I can now reconstruct his line of thought from my better understanding of his views. It was a painful experience, almost as if I had been shown up publicly to be committing a crime. Jimmy's arguments made me see with humiliating clarity how wide a gap there was between my declared values and my teaching; it was radically to change my future work with sixth forms. Three or four years later I had completely changed my views, and believed that a class of students can be helped to work together and with their teacher to develop a *response* to whatever book they are reading and that the teacher should not try to hand over to pupils a ready-made adult reading. (It is significant that for LATE *response* was the significant term, in place of the Cambridge term *discrimination*. One of my colleagues at Leeds used later to become furious if anyone used "response" in this way, for he associated the term with the idea that English teachers should value the untutored readings and interpretations of literature that pupils achieved. In contrast he wanted to emphasise the incompetence of the young who needed to be instructed in the significance of what they read. "Response" implied an evaluation of the part to be played by students in literature lessons that he found entirely unacceptable.) This collaborative view of how young people can best be helped to learn to read literature had already for some years informed my teaching of literature to non-examination forms: now I could assert it as a universal principle.

Many of the new principles that were to influence my teaching at Minchenden came from Jimmy Britton, usually from his public lectures at the Institute of Education, for it was very unusual for him to take a strong line during an LATE meeting, as he did in reply to my Leavisite approach to the teaching of literature. However, I must not underestimate the influence of other members of LATE, not only the support of prominent ones such as Nancy Martin but also the effect of spending so much time with many liberal-minded teachers who were sharing the kind of learning that I was experiencing. Both during meetings and in a bar afterwards we talked and talked about our work and the new understandings that were becoming available. For example, I understood already that mere exercises in writing would be ineffective ways of helping young people to improve. A simplistic way of characterising some of the changes of emphasis would be to say that both in literature and in what we continued to call "language" – that is, writing and other uses of language that did not involve literature – helping pupils to develop what they could do and understand, took precedence over the transmission of values and skills. But the changes went further: the next step after acknowledging the validity of pupils' responses to poetry was to see that pupils' writing too should engage with those aspects of life that genuinely mattered to them in their lives outside school as well as inside. What we called "personal writing" was moving to the centre of English teaching. At first the emphasis fell upon the topics selected, and the principle that the English teacher as the main reader of what was written should provide a sensitive and understanding audience. Implicit in the latter was the further principle that we should *reply* to the ideas and experiences that our pupils wrote for us, rather than merely *evaluate* them. After all, who will trust someone with their innermost thoughts and feelings if in response all they will receive are judgements of the means used, while no interest is shown in the content?

It may have been at about this time that English teachers began to use the word *stimulus* to refer to the use of poems, stories and other literary pieces as starting points when we wanted pupils to write. The use of the term was strikingly inappropriate because in the area of experimental psychology from which it was taken it implied that the response would be *determined* by the stimulus, and it was being used to refer to writing in which the writer's individual contribution was highly valued. I would have said that at Minchenden we did not talk about using literary passages as a stimulus, so it was a surprise to find a paper in which I did use the word. Whatever we called it, most English teachers fell into the practice of starting a lesson by reading prose or poetry, having classes discuss it and carry out various tasks in relation to it, and then ending by asking for writing that in some way related to it. One way of eliciting writing that was popular in LATE during these years was to play music and ask pupils to write about anything that the music suggested to them, a device that seemed to free them from uncertainties about subject matter and encourage inventiveness. I remember that I had particular success with a piece of music by Anton Berg. When he died Berg had not quite completed his opera *Lulu*, and the last act existed mainly as notes for an orchestral score, though in one part the vocal line existed as a haunting wordless lament high in a female voice. I recorded a broadcast performance, which included a scream and a shot that Berg had already written in, and played this section of the last act to several of my classes in the third and fourth years as a starting point for writing. In spite of the unfamiliar musical idiom it proved to be powerfully evocative. In retrospect I can see that in my appreciation of my pupils' writing (for example, in response to music) my criteria of approval had remained up to that time almost exclusively literary. At a meeting of LATE in April 1964 we discussed the range of *stimuli* for writing that might be used in the new CSE examination, as an improvement on the list of titles usual in GCE examinations. Those proposed included (a) an object such as a pumpkin or a glove, (b) improvised drama, (c) the showing of a clip of film, (d) poems or prose, (e) pictures, or (f) music. At one time or another I used all of these except the object and the film. Members of LATE often detached themselves from the more extreme practices by calling them "kipper sniffing", though I do not know whether odours had indeed ever been used. (One textbook author had laid himself open to mockery by advocating the lighting of a fire in the classroom wastepaper basket.)

The mere use of a *stimulus* was not in itself of great value; it was rather the discussion of possibilities and the sharing of first drafts that were important, since they provided a context for the writing, avoiding the "writing from cold" that LATE had long opposed. The discussion and other activities in the lesson helped the pupils to see possible lines to follow in their writing. I think that we were less aware that they also indicated the kinds of writing that would be acceptable, not so much the style – that would have been too much to expect – but a perspective on experience, a tone of voice. It is only now that I realise that this represents a change from my earlier practices. In the first form at Ruabon, for example, it is clear that I drew my pupils' attention to the details of poetic language, and used the blackboard to encourage them to select effective phrases for their own use in writing. In the lesson at Minchenden that HMI Mr Adams saw, I set small writing tasks, a few sentences long, in preparation for longer pieces of writing. It seems probable that the use of literature as *stimulus* militated against detailed teaching of the skills of writing, setting up instead implicit global expectations about the topics, styles, and attitudes that would be appropriate, without giving help with detail. The writing of some students blossomed magnificently under this treatment, but I now wonder whether I may not thereby have withdrawn from others some support that they might have benefitted from. Since most of the passages chosen for this purpose were literary this narrowed the range of writing that was attempted. English text books ceased to provide language and other exercises, and became collections of short prose and verse passages to be used "as a stimulus for writing". Some of these collections – such as *Reflections*, prepared by teachers in the English department at Walworth School, all members of LATE – had for many years a great influence on how English was taught. In Minchenden, however, we did not use such books, since like our friends at Walworth we took the view that as English teachers we should be selecting passages for our own use. Many of my poetry books still have pencilled annotations which indicate poems that I thought might be appropriate to share with pupils, and I remember also selecting passages from novels, from newspapers and from *The Listener*. The practice continued for many years, and did become mechanical in the hands of some teachers. Indeed, it may still survive for all I know.

Teachers do not always know of their successes, but occasional chances throw momentary light. Some years after Mr Adams' visit three girls from that class came to see me at the end of the fifth year, after the examination. They told me that they had continued for three years the poetry writing that they had begun in my lessons, and they offered me a bundle of poems to read which they had written for one another. None had seemed to be outstanding pupils, but clearly my judgement was at fault, for I met one of them again after nearly twenty-five years, and found that under her married name she was the author of an influential book on how to teach reading by using real books in primary schools.

LATE by the sixties was firmly committed to comprehensive education, and many of the teachers active in it were working in London comprehensive schools. It had become commonplace that our task was to teach all children equally. Education should be for all: we should not be presenting a programme that for one reason or another excluded a large part of the population from full participation. In 1963 or 1964 I was elected to the panel of teachers in Middlesex who were planning the English elements in a new public examination, the Certificate of Secondary Education, which was intended to provide a qualification for a much larger proportion of fifth year pupils than were able to gain a pass in the GCE. Our failure to educate adequately so many children from working class homes was a source of profound dissatisfaction for many liberal-minded teachers, and during those years there seemed likelihood of success if some radical changes were made, including the provision of comprehensive schools, new curricula and new examinations. The coming of the CSE examination provided an opportunity to change the English curriculum and how it was taught, and I spent many hours both in planning and in committee meetings struggling to set up an examination that would encourage rather than inhibit the kind of teaching that I believed in. At that time, along with other members of LATE, I was in favour of examination syllabuses that did not compel the separation of English from history, geography, social studies and so on, for at that time some schools were experimenting with cross-curricular courses, so I was disappointed when it was decided to retain strict subject divisions in the new examinations. It is interesting to recognise that in spite of our lip-service to this principle my colleagues and I were not involved in any such experiments.

Within English, LATE members had been wondering for some time whether the stories we read with pupils were so firmly embedded in middle class contexts that urban working class children were finding it hard to see them as relevant to their lives. It must have been in 1961 that LATE committee, no doubt because of the success of *Twentieth Century Short Stories*, asked me to chair a group that would collect stories for a second school anthology, this time aimed not at students taking the General Certificate of Education but the new Certificate of Secondary Education. We had to choose stories suitable for a much larger proportion of the young people at school. This selection was to be published in 1963 as *Short Stories of Our Time*; it was much used for thirty years, and is still in print in 1999. It was clear that many English teachers wanted stories that came closer to their pupils' lives, at least as the teachers' imagined them. I do not remember that my position in a selective school gave me much sense of guilt, though by the time I left Minchenden I was fully convinced of the value of comprehensive schooling, and no longer accepted the meritocratic view of education that I had gained from my father. All students were now equally important.

The priorities for the new volume of short stories were made clear during the committee's discussion. Children from working class urban backgrounds were too often expected to make sense of stories that depended for their effects on insight into the values and behaviour of the middle classes, so we looked for short stories that either reflected the urban environment, or presented generic experiences that could leap the cultural gap. This was of course quite different from the priorities of the grammar-school-oriented *Twentieth Century Short Stories*. Suitability for close study was still a require-ment, though relevance to pupils' lives was seen as a more important criterion than quality alone. In spite of the fact that my own school was a grammar school I happily accepted the task, and indeed with the other members of the group tried out on my own pupils many of the stories that were put forwards for possible choice. The shift of focus is made clear in the introduction to the new volume.

> Most of the stories in this book are set firmly in a twentieth century urban milieu, and they deal with aspects of the life that is confronting their young readers ... They offer many opportunities for the kind of discussion that moves out from the text into life ... For the teacher this provides the most rewarding way of helping his pupils to give body to the words of the story, to re-create it out of their own experience. After such discussion the pupils return to the story with a fuller awareness of its relevance to them and of its relationship with the reality they know.

This conception that attention to the work of literature and discussion of related aspects of the readers' lives might contribute to one another through interaction was an important strand in my thinking that was eventually to become part of the idea of "the classroom conversation" (though discussing that must be postponed until later).

It is impossible to tell whether the reading, discussion and trial lessons in preparation for *Short Stories of Our Time* generated a change in my teaching. As the years passed I had found that I was selecting poems and prose passages that impinged upon aspects of life that my pupils seemed to find important. Some were of public importance such as attitudes to members of other ethnic groups or the impact of war on people, and others were personal, such as dealing with the experience of anger and dispute within a family. What probably began as a device to earn the attention and interest of adolescent pupils later led to a sense that there was an urgent group of social and moral topics to be explored. My teaching was no longer based upon the belief that there was a corpus of *important literature* to be shared, but rather that there were issues all about us to whose understanding our shared reading and discussion would contribute significantly. My preconceptions had switched from a reified version of culture to a culture that inhered in interpersonal and social interaction, and the active meanings that they generated. I was ready for Vygotsky and his views. All round us were urgent social and ethical topics that my pupils ought to be thinking about, and literature provided a valuable entry into them. It was later argued that English teachers of our generation turned literature into sociology, but that was to misrepresent our practice. Novels, plays and poems were appropriate precisely because they enacted in a personal and dramatic form what true sociology handles abstractly and without passion. I am told that in music and the visual arts it is often possible to discuss *form* without reference to the world about us, but it was my opinion that analyses of the form of a novel or the verse forms of poetry were irrelevant to adolescents' attempts to grasp what the works have to offer. The formal analysis that I had met in my reading had sought to show patterns in character, events and plot in the novel, and concentrated on prosody, stanza form, and figures of speech in verse. I believe that more recent approaches to literary form have, for example, asked why a writer has made particular choices, an approach which seems of great value. Indeed, many of the questions that I asked my older pupils to consider were of that kind, though I would not have considered them to be questions about "form". To respond explicitly to works of literature is to deal with meaning, and that implies relating the literature in one way or another either to our lives, the source of so many of the meanings that we have available, or to some other cultural source. So I found myself placing increasing emphasis on helping pupils of all ages to link the works of literature that they were reading with the lives they were experiencing and the public events that they read about. I do not believe that I ever chose a work of literature because it threw light on the period when it was written. Such a choice would have been unimaginable in the light of the values that were guiding my colleagues and me.

I have already mentioned that the LATE working party that I helped to chair in the mid-fifties took exception to the current practice of requiring examination classes to focus detailed attention on no more than three works of literature, for it was this that led to the publication of *Twentieth Century Short Stories*. Even as early as 1955, members of LATE thought that close study should be accompanied by the reading of a wider range of literature. The terms *intensive* and *extensive reading* were used by James Britton in a lecture he gave at that time. It was not only LATE, of course, that endeavoured during several decades to move literature teaching away from the authoritative transmission of *the right reading* of a few works. When I was at

Minchenden in the sixties this bore further fruit in the practice of providing *short sets* for each class, that is, perhaps five copies of each of six titles, usually fiction but not always. (For older classes we included occasional titles of popular sociology which were being published in paperback – *Family and Kinship in East London, The Acquisitive Society,* and *The Lonely Crowd* are titles that come to mind.) These were books for the pupils to read without direct guidance from a teacher. Pupils were encouraged to read them in their own time, partly by a choice of books they would be likely to enjoy, and partly by occasionally giving time for group discussions of whichever book they were currently reading, or sometimes by requiring them to write about one of the books. I was never entirely convinced of the value of this, though it certainly helped those pupils who were already keen readers to obtain suitable books more easily. I was more convinced of the value of having sixth form pupils write about books of their own choice, and they sometimes chose to write about a book from a *short set.*

A major difference at Minchenden was the fact that I was now leading a department of some size, for at Ruabon only one of my colleagues was teaching English. We were never more than six or seven in all, but there was clear need for me to offer some kind of leadership. The development of a set of values to guide our teaching owed a great deal to my colleagues, especially Dennis Roberts and Yvonne Redman (now Bradbury). Later we were joined by Robert Hardman, Elizabeth Stuttard (now Hardman) and others. Because of my links with the lecturers at the Institute of Education our work became increasingly visible as the years progressed and visitors, both groups of teachers in training and dignified overseas visitors, were sent to see us teach. As the years passed the department became tightly knit, meeting to discuss policy and joining in LATE activities. Yvonne Redman in particular was an enthusiastic member of LATE and I benefited greatly from opportunities to discuss the new perspectives with her and how to put them into practice. The department met fairly frequently, sometimes at school and sometimes in my home, and at these meetings we worked together to formulate policies, taking turns to introduce discussion on each part of the curriculum we were responsible for. I duplicated reports of what had been decided during our meetings and each colleague had copies which were to be kept in a ring file, where revisions could easily be substituted. The idea was that our policies were not to be frozen but open to continual change as our discussions progressed: I called it "a rolling syllabus". I remember that when an American, Jim Squire, then secretary of the large and powerful National Council of Teachers of English, visited the school he laughed aloud at the idea of a curriculum statement that was in process of change. For him, and probably for many American educators, curriculum was something that was laid down authoritatively, usually from above, and at that time in the form of statements of objectives. From that perspective our rolling syllabus was comically imprecise and vague. Undoubtedly we depended on phrases (such as "response" or "personal development") that had not been formally defined, but that does not mean that we had not developed common procedures for putting these apparently vague ideas into practice.

I would like to be able to show how my teaching was influenced by my colleagues, for I am sure it was, perhaps as much in informal exchanges in the staff room as during departmental meetings, serious though those were. There was a group of younger teachers who sat together during lunch-time, not only teachers of English but of history, geography, and classics and at times others. We shared liberal views of teaching and provided powerful support for new ideas as well as a forum where we could share successes and failures. Dennis Roberts remembers this as the time when we were learning at LATE that talking and writing is an essential part of learning, not only in English but in all parts of the curriculum, because it is the way in which we gain access to our own thinking and begin to take some responsibility for it. For other (non-English) members of the group it provided a milieu in which teaching could be discussed, failures and successes acknowledged, and support given. A young geography teacher, Margaret Bradley (now Roberts), was encouraged by our talk about collecting prose and verse for use in English lessons to look out beyond the standard geography texts for material for her work, and this led her towards some very innovative teaching. (I can still remember some of the striking written work done by her pupils in geography.) In the staff room we talked about our teaching but also about a wide range of other topics, including political events such as the Cuban missile crisis.

The collaboration of the younger English teachers was naturally of particular importance to me: we shared ideas for poems and short stories to read with our classes, and even at times combined classes for team teaching, particularly of drama. When I was still uncertain about drama teaching I gained greatly from teaching with a young student teacher who had taken a qualification at a college of drama. I knew how to manage a class and organise a lesson and he knew how to teach drama, so we learnt a great deal from one another by team teaching. My younger colleagues encouraged me in further innovation, rather than putting any brake upon it. I remember particularly that a number of the stories included in *Short Stories of Our Time* were suggested by Yvonne Redman, who had tried them with her classes. Another form of collaboration with colleagues in the department arose from our policy of spending our funds on works of literature and not upon textbooks. We wanted our lessons to be fresh and relevant to the issues of our time, so we decided that we should for the most part choose our own materials and invent tasks for the pupils. We spent a good deal of time in meetings and informally in discussing activities for use in lessons, but we also made a collection of poems and passages of prose which we duplicated using the crude but invaluable *Banda* spirit duplicator. These might be read for their own sake or form the springboard for a writing task set to the students. Each of us after using a bundle of duplicated papers in a lesson, perhaps containing a group of poems, an extract from a novel or part of a newspaper article, placed them on a shelf in the departmental room so that they would be henceforth available to other members of the department, and thus we built up an invaluable resource for every English teacher who wanted to use it. The department's use of a small room in the old house that was at the centre of Minchenden School was a great boon.

Part 2

The Later Years

6 Teaching the Fifth Forms

During the years at Minchenden all of my teaching changed. I found ways of devolving responsibility so that my pupils of all ages played a more active part in their learning. In teaching literature, for example, I still led class discussions but as the years passed I gave the students more and more opportunities to develop their own attitudes and thoughts through discussion in small groups as a preliminary to bringing them to the forum of the whole class. I found that this made the more hesitant students more confident, and helped all students to develop their thought more systematically. This was particularly true in the sixth forms, which were large at Minchenden.

I am able to describe in more detail my teaching during the latter years at Minchenden because of articles that I wrote at about this time. This section deals with the teaching of pupils in the year of the leaving examination, though at Minchenden most of them were likely to remain at school for another two years, entering the sixth form to obtain further qualifications. This narrow focus comes from the existence of a published article which gives much detail about my teaching of these classes in the last few years at the school. *English in the Examination Fifth Form*, was published in two parts in *The Use of English* in 1968, two years after I had left the school. [I shall call it *the fifth form paper* to avoid repeating the whole title.] It originated in a talk that I was invited (probably by Nancy Martin) to give at the London Institute of Education, probably in 1965. I used the same talk elsewhere once or twice, and on one occasion Frank Whitehead – by then Senior Lecturer at Sheffield University – was present, and it was he who recommended to Denys Thompson, the editor of *Use of English,* that a version of it should be published in that journal, though by that time my practice and my beliefs had moved well away from the Cambridge values that the journal usually promulgated. Although the paper gives a very detailed snapshot of the best aspects of my school teaching as it came to an end and offers a justification of them, unfortunately it shows little of the history of how I reached there, but I have in some degree supplied that from memory. By this time I was enjoying teaching younger pupils more than the examination forms, so it seems probable that my teaching of them was at least as inventive, and probably more coherent since I was free of the constraints of examinations.

My belief was that in the Fifth Year English teachers should see their task as encouraging their pupils to use language to explore experiences of importance to them, in the confidence that this would develop their language abilities. Rather than spending time preparing for the examination, fifth year pupils should become involved in a wide variety of language uses, planned and carried out by themselves alone or in groups, with one another for audience, and dealing with topics which they have helped to choose. The idea was that the students would be more likely to develop the language skills needed in the examination – as well as in their lives – through talking, reading and writing about topics that they were interested in, than by repetitious practice of typical examination tasks which were often no more than decontextualised exercises. Whether this was the case is, of course, open to debate. Examinations, because of their brevity, tend to test at best a narrow range of language abilities, at worst engaging with no more than some of the surface aspects of language use, and these can often be developed as isolated skills.

To achieve this range of uses of language I put forward the concept of *"the classroom conversation"*, a view of how communication between teacher and class and between the pupils of a class should ideally be managed. The concept had been developed by a working party of LATE members which I convened to discuss poetry teaching. There was a danger that the unfamiliar feelings and language of the poems found in school anthologies made them seem to many pupils to be irrelevant to their needs and interests. However, if poetry could be thought of as merely one kind of personal language, parallel in kind and intention with prose literature and anecdotal talk, though more closely woven, it could take its place in teaching more easily and be more acceptable to pupils. In the course of classroom conversation about a topic it would be possible for a poem to be introduced as the expression of another viewpoint. The stress in English lessons would fall upon what experience – real or literary – meant to the pupils, so that the talking and writing became a sharing of real attitudes and experiences. Teacher and class would talk and write not about 'what we ought to say in the examination' but about 'what you think about it, 'why I see it differently', 'what happened to me once', 'what it seemed like in the story'. It was no longer the work of literature that was defining the frame of reference for what was to be talked and written about; "the story" appears in those phrases as if an afterthought. The concept of a classroom conversation owed something to a paper by Michael Oakeshott called 'The Voice of Poetry in the Conversation of Mankind' which Harold Rosen had mentioned to me, and also to the seminars that some members of the group were having with Michael Halliday. (The seminars were part of *The Schools Council Programme in Linguistics and English Teaching* which under Halliday's leadership set out to explore what linguistic theory might contribute to the teaching of the English in schools. The conviction that we learn from discussion is more likely to have come from members of the group such as Peter Doughty, also a member of LATE, than from Halliday himself, I suspect.) By this time, spoken language had moved into the centre of our thinking about English, and it had become commonplace in LATE to refer approvingly to "talk", though it still needed justification for other audiences. It was necessary to explain to other teachers that we were using the word 'talk' rather than 'speech' to make it clear that what was in question was not a special activity like a lecture but a normal human exchange which could continue outside the classroom. At times (we said) it would display an analytical bent which would justify the word 'discussion' but at other times it could allow the frankly personal and anecdotal. We acknowledged the importance of the teacher's part in the discussion, in asking central questions, in insisting on further exploration, yet we believed that the more unobtrusive it was the better. This dynamic and interactive view of classroom communication naturally has important implications for learning and how learning activities should be set up. It was as if we were moving towards Bakhtin's ideas long before we had ever heard of him. However, I don't think we ever spelt out to ourselves at that stage that meaning is not just a matter of individual consciousness but is created in the course of dialogue between members of a group as they sort out what they are trying to do and how they are doing it. We were still partly trapped within the psychological individualism of earlier decades, influenced by Piaget and others.

The classroom conversation united the study of literature and the activities called *language* which included writing on non-literary topics. At that time the different aspects of the English curriculum were still often treated as quite separate, as I had done during my earliest years of teaching. My colleagues and I were aware that to unite them – in a way that later became commonplace – was then quite innovative. The idea of the classroom conversation always included the principle that poems and other works of literature should enter the conversation as if they too were voices, so that literature and *language* would coexist. This did not mean that other aspects of language teaching were omitted. Pupils' written work was corrected, and time in lessons given to discussion of writing and some of the problems that pupils met in the course of writing. However, much of the work throughout the year was language and literature at once: not only LATE and NATE but many other English teachers were moving strongly in that direction. This was closely related to the conviction that our uses of language should be not treated as skills to be dealt with out of the context of pupils' current writing, because they were seen to be too deeply embedded in the personality to be a mere superficial addition. That now seems to me an excessively romantic view, and I would now advocate rather more direct attention at least to those skills that can be directly taught. I am not here thinking of spelling and punctuation which have some importance but should not be allowed to dominate young people's attention when they write. Even less am I thinking of little "grammar exercises" – putting words into boxes or correcting minor shibboleths. The skills that can and ought to be taught are the skills of ordering one's thoughts, of reconsidering what one has written and finding ways of improving it, of attending in detail to the tone and implications of what one writes. These skills are difficult to teach directly since they are not needed before or after but *during* the act of writing. It is probably through discussion while pupils are writing that they can best learn how to be at once writers and critical readers of their own work. (More recently the term *conferencing* has been used in North America.) During those years, however, we aimed to set up a classroom context in which the kinds of writing that we valued would be learnt implicitly through the reading, talking and writing that constituted the classroom conversation. That holistic approach to writing has its virtues as can be seen from the pieces that I shall quote later but it would have been better combined with more direct help of the kind that I had given my pupils at Ruabon.

It has been suggested recently that English teachers of my generation were wrong to attempt to unite language and literature. It is true that the uses of language that our students will require as adults are very wide, and are often more closely related to other subjects of the curriculum than to English. There was, however, little sign that most of our colleagues teaching other subjects thought that their responsibility included helping their pupils to read, talk and write appropriately and effectively. Indeed, it was not unknown for the less thoughtful of them to blame English teachers for their pupils' failure to write about science or history topics in a well-ordered and well-expressed fashion. At that time it seemed to all concerned that *language* was as much the English teacher's responsibility as was literature, though it was far less clear exactly what was contained within that responsibility.

In the classroom conversation works of literature would stimulate exploration in talk and writing of the pupils' experience, real and imaginary, and this in turn would feed their response to literature. We held the view that in the examination year the reading of literature should not be confined to the syllabus: poems other than those set should be read, especially ones with a sharp appeal to our pupils' world. The war in Vietnam was an important topic at the time, so that a reference to it in one lesson was followed in the next by a reading of D.J.Enright's *Brush Fire*, which raised in a dramatic way how major powers worked out their rivalries through battles fought by the citizens of other countries. The focus of the poem can be gathered from the first and last sections:-

> In a city of small pleasures,
>   small spoils, small powers,
> The wooden shacks are largely burning.
> Bodies of small people lie along the shabby streets,
> An old palace is smouldering.
> Wheeling bicycles piled with small bundles,
> Families stream away, from north to south,
> From south to north...

... They know what is happening. None of them
   asks why –
They see that foreign tanks are running off
   with native drivers,
Foreign howitzers are manning native gunners –
As they pass by burning houses, on their way
   to burning houses.
Among such small people, the foreign shells
Make ridiculously big noises.

Reading this poem led to a discussion of political and ethical issues that went far beyond the bounds of the poem itself. It was in this sense that the poem became a "voice" contributing to the conversation. The principle of the class-room conversation implied that the teacher's role should be responsive rather than directive, taking account of the students' interests and needs as they become clear during lessons. Many of the examples given in the *fifth year* paper suggest that this is an idealised view, and that in fact I took a much more proactive part in seeking out starting points, literary and other, which would catch my students' interest. My colleagues and I found poems and prose passages from our own reading, sometimes from books and sometimes from magazines or Sunday papers, and typed them for duplication and use in our lessons. I detect in this engagement with social and political issues a by-product of the wider cultural changes that I have already referred to. Those years were characterised by an increasing interest in sociology and politics, and much public engagement espe-cially of young people in the politics of dissent, particularly in reference to war and nuclear weapons. We certainly did not attempt to transmit our political views to pupils but we believed that they needed to be aware of public issues and to discuss them. Was it naive and romantic to want to help older students to under-stand and participate in the adult life that was only a year or two ahead of them? In any case, schooling and the world outside were coming closer to one another. Of course, even to set up discussion of public events was a political act in that it implied that I wanted to foster a critical attitude; but then so would it have been a political act to avoid doing so. In that sense education is inescapably political.

By now I had become very aware how every teacher creates in his or her lessons a context for pupils' talk and that the part I played in the classroom conversation inevitably influenced my pupils' uses of language there, since it went far to shape their perception of the purposes of discussion and their own possible roles in it. This led to a more self-critical view of my teaching. When pupils did not join in discussion it seems that I did not immediately blame their attitudes or abilities, but rather questioned my own methods. My advice to other teachers provides an insight into the self-questioning that I was engaged in at that time.

When normal children do not talk we should perhaps ask ourselves: 'Is the topic (or the book) suitable? Am I joining in properly, and asking helpful questions? Do I listen attentively when they reply, because I am really interested in their replies, or am I just going through the motions of questioning? Is the whole class too large a group for the more uncertain adolescents to take risks in talking about matters they have not yet sorted out for themselves? ... Are they assuming that there is a "right answer" that they ought to know, and if so whose fault is it? Have I succeeded in building up an atmosphere for the frank sharing of interests, attitudes and experiences, free from heavy adult censoriousness?

I believed that any of these could hamper the growth of the classroom conversation, out of which all the other activities were to grow. It was typical of my perspective at that time that my account of the "classroom conversation" begins with the how rather than the why. Teaching encourages teachers to think in an essentially pragmatic way: the action comes long before its justification. Of course, their current expectations of teaching, of their pupils, and of the curriculum all play a part in the actions they choose to take, but this influence is often less than fully conscious – shaped by those preconceptions that Donald Schon calls "theory in action".

Written work was to arise from the classroom conversation, which would provide a context for it, though literature would still play its important part since it too was one of the voices contributing to the conversation: so ran the theory. This would certainly avoid the blunder of expecting students to write well *from cold*, which Jimmy Britton had brought home to us so forcibly in 1955. Many quite able pupils who wrote well on matters of personal interest, found considerable difficulty in managing an essay on an impersonal topic. I believed that what they lacked were the years of talk that have provided adults not only with material, but also with an imaginary audience which can be summoned up to prompt the writer with arguments and criticisms. "Our pupils, when they face a blank sheet of paper, are more alone than we are, less surrounded by voices", I wrote. Nowadays I don't think that is so: their problem is more likely to be that they aren't sure which of the voices they dare listen or respond to.

I no longer thought it helpful, as I had when I was teaching at Dartford, to set fifth year pupils each week typical examination essay topics to write about. I wanted to encourage my pupils to write about whatever mattered to them, whether it be stories, personal anecdotes, introspection, burlesque, anything they could write with passion and vitality. My way of putting it was that they were to "use language to explore their own worlds, not to serve up pre-cooked meals." We had come to realise that school students are not just preparing for living: they *are* living. Their writing need not be merely preparatory but can – *should* – engage with the issues that currently concern them. In spite of these high-minded principles I have no doubt that as the time of the examination approached I gave my pupils opportunities to practise within the expected conventions of examination "essays". I no longer believed that the central task of English was to pass on to the young the accumulated cultural riches of our literary traditions, but I still believed that it could help young people enter more fully into their lives, but now their own reading, writing and talking was at the centre of the learning. Nevertheless, I am sure that my teaching was still heavily influenced by literature, and the desire to share it with my pupils, whether I knew it or not.

It was during discussion at LATE that I came across the concept of "a framework of choice" as a way of thinking about how to help students with their writing, and this fitted well within the classroom conversation. The underlying idea was that we are not free to choose unless we can imagine a range of alternatives. Many pupils see the central requirement of school writing as a matter of fitting in with some pattern to be supplied by the teacher ; essentially they ask, 'What does he (or she) want?' so that if a teacher says to them, 'Write about anything you like' they are sent into a panic. The classroom conversation would be the means of helping them by opening the possibilities of the topic and displaying a potentially interested audience. Most important of all it would reveal to the pupil that his or her own feelings, thoughts and experiences, all summoned up by the shared exploration, are valuable in themselves, and that there is no need to defer to external requirements. I suspect that this account of the classroom conversation may give a somewhat idealised picture of my English lessons during my last few years in school teaching, but in that very supportive mixed grammar school in North London I found such conversations possible with many of my classes, even though I was unobtrusively managing much of what went on. What is most important about this passage is that it enshrines a view of English in which literature is no longer providing the context. In theory *the classroom conversation* deals with whatever range of topics the pupils can be persuaded to interest themselves in, or introduce for themselves, and it is those topics that provide the framework for the reading of literature, not vice versa. An important shift of focus was taking place, though I do not seem to have been conscious of it at the time. However, some episodes from lessons that I described in the article suggest that literature was still providing the starting point, even though it did not define the limits of what was discussed.

Classroom talk can help students to write about personally charged experiences though this depends in part upon "building up in the class a sensitivity and respect for others", I wrote. One fifth year class (fifteen and sixteen year olds) read two stories (Lawrence's *Odour of Chrysanthemums* and Katherine Mansfield's *Daughters of the Late Colonel*, – both from *Twentieth Century Short Stories*) and several poems about war, including Owen's *Dulce et Decorum Est*. The class talked only obliquely about some of the disturbing areas of experience related to these works; most of the discussion was concerned with exploring the implications of death in the stories and poems, but we did talk about visiting relatives in hospital, and about our reactions to other people's suffering. Afterwards I asked the class to write for homework about any aspect of what we had been talking about and in any way. In a sudden panic I added, 'Or about anything else you like', for not long before a girl in the class had died in a road accident outside the school and some of the boys and girls had been very shaken. Though most of the talking came from members of the class, I'm sure that it was my remarks, questions, and responses to the students' contributions that made the running, and elicited much of what was said. I didn't set the discussion up to deal with death and people's feelings about it, but gladly accepted it when the talk moved in that direction. The writing that came from this sequence of lessons was very pleasing, in that many students did deal sensitively with this difficult area of experience, a few even writing about dying relatives or the dead classmate. I certainly did not see my work with pupils as psychotherapeutic, as a few rash English teachers seemed to suggest at this time, but I was concerned to encourage them to think and feel – and of course, write – about aspects of our common experience that were important to them. One poem particularly pleased me; it was written by a boy of very considerable ability:

UNCLE DIED

Uncle is dead.

Johnny and I remember,
when we were younger and lived over the shop,
the Sunday rides.

The mumbles, stumbles
cough and spit.
The tight muffler, the Woodbines that made
the phlegm-sea tickle and splash.

But we moved. Uncle became a fat obstacle,
parked in the largest armchair,
slippered, immune from sense and sensation,
gravy-stains on his waistcoat, fag-ash.
A burbling, semi-domesticated animal, another piece of furniture.

Sometimes he would wake and gibber Yiddish
till we called Dad
and he would tell Uncle that he must
speak English so that the kids could understand.

Uncle shrugged—and went back to sleep.
Uncle is dead,
there's no gap, no aching hole,
nothing.

Dad says we're all a bloody sight better off.
Is Uncle?
He could only be partly conscious of his own existence,
Sleeping when he was awake.
He never laughed at the T.V.
It was in English.

Indeed it is a brilliant piece for a fifteen or sixteen year old to have written, but did I then see it for what it is? At that time, like other members of LATE, I valued my pupils' writing most highly when they wrote directly about their lives, exploring the texture of experiences and their feelings about it, and was less pleased by writing that was skilful but obviously derivative. I can see now that *Uncle Died* is far from being an exploration of first-hand experience, though some of the themes it touches on were probably relevant to its author's life. Was I deceiving myself, caught up in a set of expectations that prevented me from seeing what was before me? The poem is a brilliant piece of artifice, and none the worse for that. It has to be read more in relation to other works of literature and to the non-literary myths which help to shape our lives than to what I would expect to have been the boy's first-hand experience. Looking back it seems to me that I was seeing my pupils' writing through expectations that were very powerful with most of the English teachers whom I knew in LATE. Because we believed that some pupils were not gaining full benefit from schooling because it was too far from their other cultural experiences and norms, we wanted to move their work in English closer to their real world, perhaps half-forgetting how much our "real worlds" are made up of the images and myths current in the culture we are part of. In its careful crafting, *Uncle Died* is like most published adult poems, for few are raw records of first-hand experience but representations of *created* experiences. And that is inevitable. We can neither talk nor write without responding in one way or another to the discourse of talkers and writers that have gone before, and to the images and even the phrasing typical of the cultures we witness and take part in. There is no clear-cut distinction to be made between the first-hand and the derivative. Many of the other pieces written for that homework were closer to first-hand experience, no doubt, than *Uncle Died* was, but I suspect that then and at other times most of the best pieces of writing that came from what was later to be called *the Growth model* were literary creations rather than accounts of direct experience.

Literature was still very important in my teaching in other ways, though small group discussion allowed me to shift to the students a larger share of the responsibility for interpreting works of literature. This compelled me to think about where group talk fitted into the sequence of work in a typical lesson, and how it related to my introductory presentations, to class discussion and to written tasks. Moreover, I had discovered that recordings of small group talk provided a very direct way of finding out how my pupils approached works of literature when not directed by me. Later when I was interviewed for university posts I said that I wanted to investigate young people's responses to literature, and it was something like this that I had in mind. However, events overtook those intentions.

It would be interesting to identify when it was that I realised that meaning is not inherent in the words themselves but has to be brought to them by the reader. I was aware at Cambridge of T.S. Eliot's contention that works of literature have to be recreated by each generation, but he seems not to have acknowledged that the individual reader too engages in acts of creation. This is true not only of understanding literature but for every text and utterance. From the very beginning of my teaching I had encouraged my pupils to talk about what poems and stories meant to them, but I was not quick to theorise why this might be of value to them. By 1963 or 1964 I had given some thought to the reader's role in the construction of meaning, and to what this implies for the role played by learners in making sense of poems and other works in literature lessons. I believed that the teacher should not try to hand over to his pupils a ready-made adult response. Pupils' responses need to be summoned up out of their past experiences by their own efforts; the teacher's task is to encourage this by making it possible for them to explore together what the poem, novel or play can mean to them. The teacher can contribute some of his or her own perceptions to the exploration, but it may be more important to encourage the students, at least upon first reading. My fear was that if teachers demanded "adult attitudes" and "the impersonal and formal manner of adult criticism" from their pupils this would generate insincerity and apathy. However, although I advocated "wide individual reading" the pupils were not to be abandoned to struggle alone with the more demanding texts read for examinations: the classroom conversation would enable them "to build up a class response through talk". I was thus seeing the reading of literature as a social activity; meaning would not arise solely from interaction between individual and text. The young reader's response is not created merely with the initial reading, but can be extended and deepened by sharing with others, his contemporaries as well as the teacher. This response will not be taken in and made their own by all pupils equally, but all will share it in some degree, and it will give special support to those who on their own find it hard to commit themselves to the experience of a particular poem or piece of prose. I was aware that in following this line of thought I was making recommendations that conflicted with current practice in the face of fifth year examinations, which, in my view, often interposed themselves between the teacher and a clear perception of his or her pupils' needs. Because of this, teaching the set books could easily become a meaningless drudgery. I took the view that if pupils leave the school with no memories of pleasurable discovery in the reading of literature but only a stale taste in their mouths, then their English teachers have failed, even if they have passed the examination.

It never occurred to me at that time that with older students it could be appropriate to read works of literature that were *not* likely to be relevant to pupils' experience, or ones that I thought meretricious and misleading. It has been pointed out to me that it would have been possible to read a poem such as Newbolt's *Vitai Lampada* ("There's a breathless hush in The Close tonight...") as a study of the literature, values and attitudes of a particular time and social group, in that case the poses and prejudices of upper class Englishmen in the late nineteenth century. Such a choice would have been too far from the central emphasis of our teaching, the bringing of students into *personal possession* of works of literature. I wanted the novels, plays and poems to speak to them of the human condition as they themselves were beginning to know it. A more distant and analytical understanding I would have thought appropriate only to university undergraduates. (When during my years in the Bradford school I had indeed read *Vitai Lampada* with my pupils, it was for its own sake as a poem, and not in order to place it in a socio-cultural context. It now seems amazing to me that I was willing to treat its posturing uncritically, for today such values cry out for mockery, though I had found as a young teacher that mockery however justified can discourage young people from taking any adult literature seriously.)

In approaching the texts set for the examination, I found it best to start with as quick a reading as possible in order to get a rapid overall view. In the case of plays, including those by Shakespeare, I decided in advance which scenes or parts of scenes could be omitted and summarised; which could in some sense be 'acted'. Some scenes were read and acted by the whole class in pairs or larger groups, a few scenes were read by me or by picked readers who had been warned in advance, and other scenes omitted, with a rapid summary. The purpose of this was for the class to gain an overall impression. Then followed open discussion – and by this I meant discussion and not monologue – exploring in the class' own terms what the story, poem or play meant to them. My purpose was to help them to bring up their own relevant experience to body out the work, since the meaning of a work of literature can come from nowhere else than each reader's own experience, and each reader must construct his or her own meaning at the bidding of the author's words. The discussion, which might be carried on first in small groups and then in full class, was guided by whatever in the story, play or poem the pupils had found important – or for that matter puzzling or objectionable – in the first reading. Whatever different perceptions I was able to offer had to wait until later, though I joined in the discussion in their terms.

Later in the year each work was returned to for closer attention to certain poems and key passages and scenes from novels and plays. In studying plays the students spent some time acting scenes that were likely to reward careful attention, as well as discussing their significance in the play as a whole. During my last two years at the school, I handed over the more detailed study to groups of students. The play would be divided into six or seven sections and each section given to a largish group of students to prepare over a sequence of lessons and homework. Each group would finally perform its section to the rest of the class, answering questions about details of meaning and general interpretation, and leading a discussion of the function of the section in the whole play. Some groups, I acknowledged, needed a good deal of guidance. With a novel one of the key passages was discussed first in groups, with questions on the blackboard and then by the class as a whole, but not necessarily just following my questions, since some groups, if their discussion had gone well, would raise issues that I had not foreseen. I would give to the groups questions such as these:

What's that in for?
What would *you* think if someone said that?
Whose point of view is expressed here? How do you
   know it's not the author's?
What are we meant to feel about this?
Did you expect this to happen?

Later in the discussion with the whole class I would challenge assertions with demands for evidence, in order to send the students back to search the text. As far as I can remember this pattern of questions represents my practice with reasonable accuracy. It seems to be a development from my teaching of *Passage to India* and other novels at Ruabon seven or eight years earlier, though the questions are not so strongly directed by my own reading of the text.

When reading poems I combined this approach with others, one method being to "hand over to the pupils the task of preparing a reading". For example, when approaching a group of poems set for study, the class would work in groups of about four, perhaps choosing two poems and preparing them for group reading to the class, using any methods which seemed to suit them. In choosing their own two poems from all the possibilities, discussing how to perform them, performing them and hearing the performances of other groups, they could in a double period read or hear twelve or more poems, some of them several times over, and begin to talk at their own level about meaning and interpretation. Another change of emphasis occurred when I detected in myself a desire to force my pupils to a critical response. Several members of LATE decided that we should more often just read poems to our pupils, carefully choosing ones likely to make an immediate impact. My practice was to wait for a moment to see if there was any comment, and if there was none just go on and read the next. I believe I still have a tape recorded programme of poems that I made at that time for playing to fourth form pupils. It includes at least one folk song that I sang for the programme.

Eventually as the examination approached I had to turn back to the prescribed works of literature in order to prepare more directly for the examination. Even then I felt it important to avoid projecting upon them a 'right answer' approach. It was in the class discussions after the students' group discussions that I found my contributions to be most telling, because they came as solutions to problems already half-solved by my pupils themselves. I encouraged pupils to take written notes not only of work done individually and in groups, but also of our full-class discussions, yet I still avoided dictating my own response as if it were definitive. Some pupils needed help with their note-taking, and I found it useful after a discussion to ask; 'Well, what ought we to keep of all those ideas? What have *you* got down, Geoff?' and then to move the class into a summing-up discussion, to determine which were the most significant issues which had been raised. During my years at Minchenden School I asked pupils more and more frequently first to make notes for themselves and then, using the blackboard, discussed with them which were the most important issues, and how they should be ordered. I found this valuable with younger pupils as well as with those in the fifth and sixth forms, and it often became part of the preparation of a piece of writing. The importance of note-taking goes far beyond its immediate use in, for example, preparing for a piece of writing. In schooling the taking of notes by students, and their discussion at the blackboard, can become an instrument of metacognitive reflection, of making one's own thoughts the subject of thinking, and thus one of the most powerful devices at a teacher's disposal, since it enables a teacher both to model his or her own strategies and to make the pupils' processes of reflection public and shared. Thus one of the most inward and important cognitive skills can be opened up to young people.

I seldom referred in the fifth year article to the writing that arose from the work on literature, except in relation to the first stage during which the class gained a general awareness of the work as a whole. Any written work at that early stage was either the writing of stories or poems stimulated by the reading, or general exploration of the whole work, determined by the individual pupils' interests. The general exploration was not necessarily confined to the work. Just as the conversation linked literature with life, so can the two be explored together in the same piece of writing. The critical examination of specific issues in writing was left until later, when it would arise from the more detailed study in groups. I must certainly have expected more writing to be done than is mentioned in the article. By the end of the year I would have been setting tasks indistinguishable from those that students were to expect in the examination.

In retrospect I am struck by how fully this approach to the teaching of literature is developed, though the account is undoubtedly highly selective. In spite of my advocacy of the classroom conversation, and of a framework that derives from my pupils' lives and from the public life we shared via the media, the article makes it clear that literature was still making much of the running, providing starting points for improvised drama and for discussion, as well as providing the models for so much of the writing the students did.

I must not allow the existence of a detailed account of how I was teaching the fifth year pupils to obscure the work I was doing with younger pupils. Indeed, during my last few years at Minchenden the teaching of these younger boys and girls became more interesting and more rewarding to me. For that reason I am providing here a brief counterbalance to the previous section.

It must have been in 1963 or 1964 that Minchenden School, expanding in size, acquired a disused school some distance away and located the youngest two year groups – pupils aged between 11 and 13 years – in those premises. Dorothy had taught in a school whose head teacher believed that the youngest pupils should be taught at least in part by the most experienced teachers. With this in mind, I decided, in spite of practical difficulties, that I must not allow myself to be detached from the youngest of our pupils and so arranged my timetable that I taught one second year class and one lesson per week with three of the four classes in the first year group. In that way, I reasoned, I would come to know at least three quarters of our pupils by name, and would know something of their work in English.

At first, I found, their writing was extremely inhibited, characterised by short sentences, bland statements which concealed their own view of the matter in hand, and a concern for safe "correctness" rather than engagement with the topic. My aim in reading poems and prose with them and encouraging them to talk, first about the works of literature and then about their own experiences and ideas related to the same topics was to validate their perspectives, and persuade them to take risks and be more experimental in their writing. Of course, once they became confident in the new cultural milieu presented by the grammar school they showed themselves less inhibited than some of my older students, over whom hung the doubts and suspicions of adolescence. I have already illustrated the qualities I valued when I quoted the passage called *Death of a Perch* and described the remarkable openness of that class in discussion, though by that time the class had entered on its second year.

As I saw the first year classes only once a week, my usual practice was to read something with them, to institute discussion, and then to ask for writing. I do not think that I used a group format as often as I did with other classes, but tended to lead the discussions. This was partly because I wanted to get to know the boys and girls, and partly because it seemed important to establish a habit of rational discussion in which pupils were expected to deal courteously with differences of opinion. Whatever the age of the pupils I would not tolerate scornful or dismissive behaviour to other pupils: nothing would be more destructive to the trust in sharing experience that I wanted to set up. I was delighted with much of the writing that came out of these lessons with younger children, and I was equally pleased with many of the discussions. I now greatly regret that I kept no examples of work done by first year pupils.

I began to realise that the balance of my interests had changed. I was finding the greatest pleasure no longer in teaching literature to the examination classes, but in helping younger pupils to reflect on their own experiences and to talk and write about them. I can see now that this was in line with the wider shift during a period of fifteen years or more when I had moved from seeing my central task as introducing pupils to literature to that of encouraging them to develop the use of their own language resources. In this latter task the reading of literature played an important but not dominant role.

8 Drama Teaching

In early 1966 I was invited to write a "position paper" on drama in English teaching for "The Dartmouth Seminar", a month-long international conference on English teaching that was to be held at Dartmouth College, in New Hampshire. This was in spite of the fact that at no point did I consider drama to be central to the English curriculum. Although the paper describes only lessons using drama methods it has the advantage of dealing with younger students, and shows very clearly the changes that I was making not only in drama but in the way I managed pupils' participation in lessons. A version of that paper formed part of a booklet *Drama in the Classroom* which I wrote for NCTE as one of the "outcomes" of the Dartmouth Seminar. (I was asked to create the booklet by "editing" the papers written by members of the drama working group during the seminar, but as the drama group not surprisingly talked rather than wrote there were only a few pages that I could quote, so in the end I wrote almost all the booklet.) Although this section gives dramatic work more prominence that it had in my teaching, I have retained much of the detail from that chapter because it displays many of the methods I was using in other lessons as well as the principles they were based upon.

I have confessed that I had always lacked confidence in the teaching of drama, as well as in my powers as a producer of plays for performance. Indeed, in spite of the three productions I had taken responsibility for in previous schools, I thought it fortunate that during my years at Minchenden there was always one colleague or another who wanted to take charge of school productions. However, my attitude to drama in the classroom changed because during the early sixties I began to introduce improvisation into lessons. At first my purpose was to help pupils gain more effective access to works of dramatic literature, but later I came to see dramatic improvisation as another way of representing experience, real or possible. Perhaps drama, like writing, could provide pupils with a way of exploring and making sense of their lives, and contribute to the quality of the writing, as well as being valuable in itself. In retrospect it seems inevitable that, since the main shift of emphasis during those years was towards acknowledging the pupils' concerns, it was entirely consistent for my drama teaching to become centred not on the study of plays – though that naturally continued – but on improvisation. I don't think that at the time I realised these implications.

I had seen demonstrations of drama teaching, including improvisation, in LATE meetings and elsewhere, including an exciting conference on art in education that Dorothy and I had travelled to London to take part in during our years in North Wales. The initiative for change was provided by shame that this part of my teaching was so unsatisfactory in comparison with other teachers. To improve my work I attended LATE conferences on drama teaching, and even chaired the group that organised another such conference, for I was determined to learn how to do it. I have already mentioned that I learnt a great deal from team teaching with a young drama teacher in training who spent a term on practice in the department. I had benefited from Dorothy's experience in drama and had taken ideas from books that I read, especially Brian Way's *Development through Drama* and *Teaching Drama* by R.N. Pemberton-Billing and A.B. Clegg, and eventually it became impossible to recall which ideas came from reading, which from other teachers' suggestions, and which were my own. This change in emphasis must have been well under way by November 1963 since, during an LATE meeting about using BBC Schools Programmes as stimuli for written work, I urged that pupils would write about more deeply felt experiences if they improvised scenes containing a dramatic clash of personality before writing.

To my surprise those overseas visitors who were sent by the London Institute of Education to observe my teaching were more impressed by my drama lessons than any other, perhaps because they had never seen anything similar. This was particularly true of one or two American visitors, such as Jim Squire, then Secretary of NCTE, for in the USA practical drama was not part of the English curriculum, though of course there were excellent drama teachers there. It must have been his doing that I was invited to provide the paper on drama for the Dartmouth Seminar. I had become an authority on drama without intending or meriting it.

The chapter *Initiating the Use of Drama* was focused upon ways in which an inexperienced teacher might deal with uncertainty about the teaching of drama. I had discovered that throwing pupils into the deep end by merely placing them in groups and giving them a task of improvising or preparing a written scene for presentation was useless. They needed to learn gradually how to control their embarrassment, how to manage their actions and speech so as to express meaning, and how to collaborate. In order to achieve this I suggested that work in drama should show three kinds of development over time:

(a) from teacher control to control by the demands of the task,
(b) from individual work to group and then class collaboration,
(c) from purely imitative actions to actions that express intention, attitude and personality.

The first of these seems to parallel the progress of my learning between 1961 and 1966 about the requirements of drama teaching, much of it from trial and error, for I began with tight control of the activities and only gradually learned how to hand responsibility to my pupils.

I began by devoting not more than twenty minutes to dramatic work though eventually I learnt how to continue drama work for ninety minutes without losing the pupils' concentration. As time went on I ceased to use my own classroom and moved out to the open spaces of the school hall, which was much better for practical work whether individual or in groups, even though it meant that everything that went on was highly visible to whoever moved about the school. This also enabled me more easily to collaborate with colleagues, sometimes combining two classes to work together, for it proved very useful – and not only in drama – for one teacher to manage the class and the other to notice where there were problems that called for attention. The overall pattern that I aimed at in the lessons began with the pupils under firm control. I would tell them to spread out, so that their attention was given not to one another but first to my instructions and then to the brief solo activities they were engaged in. As the students' self-consciousness and stiffness diminished, I gave them tasks that lasted longer and were less closely controlled. Later in the lesson I would give them improvisations to carry out collaboratively, first in pairs and then in larger groups. Eventually, as the groups become confidently involved in their joint tasks, they would take control of their activities while I watched them. When this did not happen I moved back to more closely controlled activities. What I was aiming for was to persuade the students so to concentrate on their own activities that the demands of the task would take control, so that I need no longer dominate but observe and intervene only when necessary.

The initial activities referred to would be designed to minimise the pupils' self-consciousness, and enable them to learn to carry out movements. To act with body and voice at once is difficult for most of us, so that it is useful to learn to manage movement in separation from speech. The tasks I chose were therefore individual, simple, and required no more than the accurate imitation of actions. The most simple imitative exercise were solo ones: lifting a pile of books from the floor to a high shelf; bending to pick up objects of various shapes, sizes and weight; writing or drawing on an enormous imaginary sheet of glass; imitating the actions of getting ready for school in the morning. Later I moved to more expressive solo activities that included, for example, approaching an imaginary dog (while I told them about the animal's reactions), or handing an imaginary wounded bird from one pupils to another. I next introduced activities that involved more movement. I had them explore different ways of walking, including wading, crossing a stream by stepping stones, walking along a narrow ledge, and groping through a dark tunnel. With younger pupils it was possible to ask them to walk "like a queen", "like a policeman", or to walk in a way that showed they were ashamed or scornful. Once the simple activities mentioned above had been achieved the work moved from individual to collaborative improvisation. This was an important stage and a difficult one, since catching another pupil's eye sometimes led to self-consciousness. With eleven-year-olds, "scorn" and "walking out in new clothes" led to "The Emperor's New Clothes"; they prepared their version of the story, working in groups of about seven or eight. "Walking on tiptoe" led to a sequence in which a group spied on a darkened house and then to a further sequence in which a class of thirteen year olds explored the dramatic possibilities of whatever they decided to find there. Finding different ways of running to a hiding place led to representing the experience of being attacked from the air, and beyond that to situations of suffering and loss in war. In this way it was possible to move from simple to more demanding and expressive tasks.

It was my main purpose to move a class into expressive tasks as soon as possible. Some of the first expressive tasks were to be done in pairs, and they included activities such as: crossing a room secretly while another person mimes unawareness and absorption in a task; a hypnotist controlling his subject's actions through his own; or a naughty urchin mimicking a pompous greengrocer setting out his wares on a stall. These were not only expressive but led naturally to the introduction of language. In the case of the greengrocer mime, I managed the transition to mime accompanied by speech by saying, "Let's do it again, but this time the greengrocer *catches* him, and we'll find out what they say to each other". All the pairs tried this, and then told the others what in fact had been said. One pair showed their version to the others, and then all the groups tried again. This was a critical shift of emphasis, the moment when the boys and girls were required to *present* their enactment to one another.

Unfortunately I no longer remember how much control I retained in such activities as entering a darkened house. Probably I kept a careful rein on the class, since it was an activity that could lead to noisy and uncontrolled behaviour that owed more to the release of tension than to an attempt to represent experience dramatically. Many thirteen year old pupils became embarrassed with realistic tasks such as walking into a coffee bar to look for a friend when everyone there is watching, and this often caused them to protect themselves by burlesquing the task. When this happened I retreated to less collaborative work in pairs before reintroducing expressive and personal elements into the tasks. As in all my teaching, my students' response to the tasks I gave them played a considerable part in shaping the policies I adopted. Useful work in improvised drama is impossible without the students' full co-operation.

As the tasks became more complex, the pairs and groups had more responsibility to organise their own activities, and this at times led to uncontrolled and exuberant action, particularly from boys. I dealt with this by slowing down the activity, either by requiring the mime to be carried out in slow motion or by controlling it with my hands and voice. With younger pupils this was represented as exercising a magic power. I said something like this:

"My hands give life to you, and you, and you, and you rise up slowly ... up, up ... always looking at me. I dart my power at you and you cower away. I draw you slowly after me against your will ... you struggle against the power ... but you have to follow. Suddenly I turn you to stone."

Other activities were designed to encourage pupils to control their movements more precisely. Older pupils moved "like a machine" first individually and then in pairs, inventing complex patterns of collaborative movement. Younger pupils acted scenes as Coppelia-like puppets, or became monsters and snakes in a formal sequence, again without touching one another. I believed that asking pupils not to touch one another meant that each "had to find a balance within himself" – or herself, of course – the idea of balance providing a metaphor for learning to tolerate conflicting feelings.

By this time I had come to believe that improvised drama could contribute to the students' personal development even before language became involved. An emphasis on the personal and particular was typical of the values of LATE at this time, which – as I have indicated – sought to bring the English curriculum close to our pupils' everyday lives. There was a strongly individualistic element in this ethic of the mid-sixties, which undervalued the social elements of communication in English, though this may not have been true of all members of LATE. Although mime had originally been introduced as a step towards the recreating of scripted plays, I had begun to attribute to it a value in its own right. Nowadays I find it difficult to ascribe a clear meaning to that phrase "personal development" except in so far as the work in drama may have helped shy adolescents to present themselves more confidently when faced with an audience. I can see that I was at that time "teaching drama" without knowing it.

Books on drama had recommended that the teacher should read a story to a class and then ask groups to prepare dramatised versions, but I had found that this led to poor work, ill-developed, unrealistic, and lacking in expressive movement, for the pupils needed preparatory guidance in analysing the episodes and finding ways of representing them. This was illustrated from lessons with a class of eleven-year-olds to whom I read an Eskimo legend *Sedna and the Hunter* from a book of folk tales. Their first attempt at improvisation made it apparent that help was needed. I asked the class to recapitulate the structure of the tale, and listed on the blackboard a sequence of scenes: a girl scornfully rejecting suitors, her flight with a mysterious lover, the storm with the seabirds who are the souls of those lost at sea, and so on. For each scene I elicited from my pupils ways of symbolising the meaning of the event, and worked with the class on expressive details for each scene, such as struggling against the force of the wind and sea, before asking the groups to prepare their versions. The three lessons given to this work ended with all the groups giving presentations.

By 1966 the emphasis in my conscious theorising had moved from the transmission to pupils of a view of the world to encouraging them to engage with the world as they experienced it. To ask pupils imitate a scene or to dramatise a story as with *Sedna and the Hunter* was to take the control of topic out of their hands, so that I looked for ways of ensuring that the subject matter of their improvisations should be of their own choosing. I wanted them to make use of any dramatic methods available in order to explore together their vision of the world in order to develop and refine it, without resort to the protection of commonplace dramatic conventions. I wanted to show them the possibilities of drama, but not at the expense of their confidence in using drama to deal with their own urgent concerns. However, avoiding the use of conventions was perhaps an unrealistic requirement. It was reasonable to discourage the introduction of stock figures such as the schoolmaster with gown and cane, and other clichés drawn from light literature, but I do not know whether I realised that no communication is possible without some use of conventional symbols. Perhaps I overestimated the extent to which my pupils were exploring their own worlds. Intelligent and often sensitive young people, they were quite capable of recognising intuitively the values that I had espoused. No doubt they set out to provide me with what I wanted. Looking back now I can see that their improvisations were often literary versions of reality, matching the *kitchen sink* literature of the sixties, which was itself an artifice for shaping a version of everyday life. They were probably influenced by film and television representations too, though I discouraged any obviously unrealistic clichés.

I was looking for ways of uniting the work of the small groups so that there would be an outcome that would involve the whole class. With a group of thirteen year old pupils I had been reading poems about leaving one's home and in particular one about refugees, so that the classroom conversation focused for a while upon national migrations and what it means to leave one's home. Then, wishing to use drama to increase their personal insight into such experiences, I took them to the school playing field and told them to divide into small groups. I said something like this: "You are refugees travelling in families across a hot and waterless desert. Decide amongst yourselves how you are related, and what kind of a person you are. Remember, you have been driven from the home where you belonged; you face possible death either here or elsewhere. How would you behave, tired and frightened, in the heat of the desert?" The groups talked for a few minutes and then tried out little incidents devised to display the personalities and relationships chosen. Later the whole class talked over the possibilities and some of the more confident groups showed the others what they had been doing. It suddenly occurred to me that we could become a tribal group without losing the family relationships. A conveniently marked area of the school field became the well they had been travelling towards, and the groups began to move towards it from the other side of the field. The leaders drew ahead and turned, encouraging the others; the strong helped the weak; family squabbles separated some groups, but others drew unity and hope from the leaders. And just as the leaders came to the well I shouted, "You discover it's empty. What do you do?" Most of the groups found an appropriate response, but then the action fell into disorder. I asked them to repeat the climax but this time to hold their pose when I clapped my hands. This final tableau was magnificent. Even though it is more than thirty years ago I can still remember the euphoria that I felt at the end of that lesson.

Speech played a major role in many of the improvisations I have already described, which had all along been planned to lead to work based upon dramatic scripts, such as the plays by Shakespeare that were studied by older students. For example, I asked a class of thirteen-year-olds to improvise in pairs, first a squabble between a man and his supercilious wife who leaves in a huff, to show a mixture of fear and determination in approaching a growling dog, and to improvise other situations closely related to the Prologue of Shaw's *Androcles and the Lion*. When these improvisations had been practised, shown to one another, and talked about, the children worked in threes upon a short section of the Prologue, acting it with scripts, putting down the scripts and improvising dialogue, watching other groups act, and discussing first the intonations and movements and then by a natural progression the nature of what was being presented. The Prologue is a slight and conventional scene, but I believed that it came to life because it was filled out with the students' own perceptions and inventions.

The main task that I gave myself was to enable pupils of from fourteen to sixteen years of age to appreciate a Shakespeare play by taking part in representing parts of it. First I wanted them to get an impression of the whole play, so having decided which scenes could be omitted or summarised I arranged a fairly rapid *run through*. Some scenes were acted in front of the class by pupils who had prepared the text, and others were acted by the whole class, as described in the previous paragraph for the play by Shaw. I tried to avoid any reading from texts that had not been looked at before the lesson, so usually pupils were asked to prepare a scene or even a single speech beforehand. Later we returned to certain scenes that were chosen because they presented situations and feelings that seemed likely to make connections with my pupils' personal experiences, and then they worked on them in detail. With older students it was often useful to set groups the task of looking at particular speeches to decide how they should be spoken. During the study of Shakespeare's *Henry V*, for example, I asked one sixth form class to work on the king's speech to Sir Thomas Erpingham before Agincourt. I wrote that "in deciding on the tones and gestures that best accounted for the pauses and changes of focus in the king's speech, they had said something about Henry's personality", but no doubt it was I who was able to make this point as a result of their work on the speech. I notice that when teachers write about their lessons, they often make it seem that part of their own contribution to a lesson came from their pupils. The mythology of elicitation is very powerful, and can even blind a teacher to what he or she is contributing to a lesson.

Detailed work on a different kind of passage can be illustrated from a lesson that introduced a younger class to the opening of *Julius Caesar*, in which members of the populace who have absented themselves from work in order to see Caesar are berated by two tribunes. (Many years before I had seen another member of LATE carrying out a similar process with younger children.) After improvising scenes in which adults were caught doing something they knew they should not, my pupils made up incidents in which trade union officials harangued unofficial strikers. Then the whole class mimed the behaviour of bystanders, and into this I introduced the two pupils who had been the most successful trade union officials, so they could berate the populace who answered insolently. Next I distributed copies of *Julius Caesar*. I cannot pretend that work on the script was an immediate success: the class had to grapple with the unfamiliar language and different tempo of Shakespeare's scene, and this required a number of repetitions in which their attention was more on the verse than their movements. It proved necessary to isolate for special attention the crowd's response to the tribunes and discuss the tone of voice implicit in the cobbler's speeches. Yet by the end of the lesson the class produced quite a commendable crowd scene, having invented most of the details for themselves. In retrospect I wonder whether this brief passage deserved the time spent on it. The best justification would be that it shows something of the public feelings and attitudes against which the political action would take place. Of course, the eventual purpose was to study the whole play, and time would not allow such detailed attention to every scene.

It was possible when preparing older students for an examination to give them far more responsibility for interpreting the text. With sixth forms – sixteen to eighteen-year-olds – I found it possible, after a first run through, to hand over large sections of the play for study by groups of pupils. Working individually and together, they spent considerable time in preparing to present their section to the rest of the class and to lead the class in discussing it. I hoped that the discussion of how to interpret details would take them towards larger issues of character and motive, and beyond that to some account of the relation of their section to the whole play. For example, a class of highly able sixth form students who were preparing *Antony and Cleopatra* for a public examination had read it through rapidly during the previous year, and seemed to have turned it into a popular fiction glorifying Love At Any Price. To help them see other aspects of the play I gave different groups various focus points, so that they could try out various scenes and then discuss them critically. With another sixth form class studying *King Lear* I chose a number of themes, such as 'The Approach of Old Age and Death' and asked groups of pupils to work on them in various ways culminating in a report back to the full class.

I had found that there was much to be gained from treating the study of literature as a joint exploration rather than the handing on of pre-digested truths. This *group investigation* can be seen as the culmination of the process through which the students became increasingly responsible for their learning activities, a change of emphasis that I shared not only with other teachers in the department but with LATE generally. When we eventually turned to texts the purpose was to enable the pupils to recreate the drama in action, at least in imagination. Grappling with the expressive demands of a play seemed as valid a way of learning to "read" it as the approaches favoured by literary criticism; at the very least it acknowledged that the work was a play and not a novel. For examination purposes it was useful that students usually became very familiar with parts of a play through finding ways of acting them..

Because so much detail is available in the NCTE booklet, I have written about my work in drama at so great a length that I have given it an importance that it did not have in my teaching. In fact drama did not take up a large proportion of the time available for English lessons. In the years after I left Minchenden I became far less persuaded of the value of improvisation to pupils' "personal development", which was the vague phrase current at the time. Nevertheless, I remain convinced that approaching a written play by representing it dramatically is an appropriate way of beginning to study it.

9   New Emphases in Writing

One important shift in English teaching during the seventeen years was a change in the kinds of writing expected of pupils. This was not just a matter of the topics chosen, but – more profoundly – of the values by which they were assessed. These values were important not merely as the basis for an assigned grade, but because the main purpose of the teaching was to communicate these values to the pupils so as to guide their writing. Like other English teachers I communicated these values in various ways: through the activities by which I introduced a writing task to a class, including the terms in which I couched it, through the preliminary reading of passages which carried implicit messages about what kinds of writing I valued, and through discussion and writing at the blackboard which simulated some of the processes of composition. After the work had been done I sometimes read aloud to the class some of the pieces they had written, and the choice of these would indicate what I valued. Occasionally I would deal with some issue at the blackboard but this would normally be a matter of warning pupils about a common error, rather than referring to the meaning and purpose of the writing done. At the end of those years I was developing occasions for having writing done for a wider audience than myself, and this implied finding some way of making the writing public, at least to the class, through such devices as pinning the pieces to a notice board. When I received the pieces written, I read and annotated them, adding a brief evaluative comment and a *mark* out of twenty at the end. This too of course carried important messages for those pupils who could use them. In earlier years I was mainly concerned to indicate errors of usage and infelicities of style, but later I came to realise that I needed to *reply* to what my pupils had written. I wanted to communicate to students that surface accuracy and conformity to expectations matter, but not to imply that they were the main purpose of learning to write. As the years went on I became more aware that I should not be expecting one unvarying style of writing, but accepted that there should be variations according to the demands of the context. A letter supposed to be addressed to a friend would not show the same characteristics as a report on an academic topic, for example. I continued to correct solecisms, but I made sure that I wrote at greater length in response to what the pupils wrote, and not usually in an evaluative mode, though I often included questions that were intended to suggest directions in which the piece might have moved with profit. I have characterised the two approaches as a dichotomy, but since the change took thirteen or fourteen years there must have been many intermediate stages.

Few records now remain of the writing tasks that I set to my pupils, but some impression of the values that lay behind the last few years of teaching writing can be gained from an examination paper that my colleagues and I set for eleven year old pupils at Minchenden. We began the rubric with: "This paper is designed to help you write well", and told them that they could write about any number of topics up to five. The topics included:

- What things in your junior school do you miss at Minchenden?
- A shopping expedition with your mother for something you don't want to have bought for you. (In prose or poetry.)
- "It was a short narrow street of tall narrow houses, and it ended in a railway embankment. I wasn't sure which house I was looking for."(Use this as the first sentence of a story or as an idea for one.)
- Write about the games you played in the playground or your junior school and about the rhymes and songs that go with them.
- Describe another adventure for Bilbo and the dwarfs to have.
- Turning out my cupboard.
- Write a letter of advice to a lady who has a niece or nephew coming to stay with her and who is worried about entertaining him/her and about what rules to make. Give advice based on personal experience.
- Your friend has consented to take care of your pet while you are away on holiday. Imagine that you are telling him (her) how to look after it. Persuade your friend that it is a loveable animal when looked after properly.
- After school one day you find that your house and family have disappeared mysteriously. The street looks the same but your house just isn't there. Describe what you felt and did.
- Write a poem or short piece of prose suggested by one of these people:-- Procrustes, The Minotaur, and Jason. (*The rubric also included identifying details for each name, and some suggestions about what might be included.*)

I did not frame all of these topics, for most of my colleagues drafted questions, but they well represent our practice in the department in about 1965. (There were three other questions, all inviting stories but giving more detailed advice.)

In general these topics illustrate our attempt to supply a context that would make explicit what our expectations were, so that we were not leaving our students to guess what was in our minds. We were clearly very ready to accept fiction: six out of thirteen questions invited stories and several others might reasonably have given rise to them. Five of the topics referred to the junior school and to family activities, such as shopping with mother – and others might be interpreted in that way – so that there was considerable emphasis upon the students' own lives or at least upon fantasies that could have been built on them. However, I have the impression that, though it was our intention to steer their writing towards the exploration of their own experience, many of our pupils preferred to write fiction. Throughout the school we encouraged the writing of verse, and in two questions this appears as an explicit possibility. Three topics are based upon fictional works that had been read during the term, but there was no attempt to test their understanding or recollection of them. Indeed, to encourage the younger children's responses to their reading we often set tasks that extended the stories they had read, for example asking them to write about the characters in other situations, the question about Bilbo (from *The Hobbit*) being an example, though rather more vague than we might have set in a lesson. However, the task that refers to the characters from stories from classical literature seems to be hoping for something different. Only the two letters required writing that was not fiction or about personal experience, and one of these seemed to require some reflection upon relationships with adults. This probably represented our policy with pupils in their first year in the school.

Many of these elements in our writing policy continued with older students, and the kinds of written work that we expected from them can be illustrated from an examination set to third and fourth year pupils (aged thirteen to fifteen). In this examination, fictional and personal writing was separated from other kinds that we had by then introduced by isolating them in separate papers. (The reason for this change is explained below.) Four of the writing tasks were based upon poems or prose passages; they were designed to reflect our practice during lessons. All the pupils listened to a tape recorded reading of a poem by D.H. Lawrence – a significant choice – and could if they wished respond in writing:-

- Write in any way you choose about anything suggested by the passage you have just heard.

The other three tasks took off from passages printed on the paper. One typical instruction ran:

- Think about the title of this poem (Philip Larkin's *First Sight*) and notice how the poet uses the idea by showing that a 'first sight' can be misleading. Make it the title of a piece of writing of your own (in prose or verse) perhaps showing more of the way in which first impressions can be dispelled; or just use the title.

The other questions included:

- Do you work for your pocket money? If so, apart from earning the money, does the job have any other interest for you? Is it one in which you meet many different people? Do you enjoy the change from school work, or is it just irksome? Choose any one or all of these aspects to write about. You will probably do better to describe a typical morning or day and (if this is relevant to your job) typical conversation.

- Spring is a subject people often write poems about. Write one rather different from the usual "lambs, flowers, pretty" sort of thing, trying to keep close to what you think is true.
- Under ground.
- Moment of madness.
- All Mod. Cons.
- A foreign city.
- Left Alone.
- Reading character from clothes.
- Write about some of the things in your past that you are proud of, or that you regret: they can be things said, done or thought.
- Describe the plot of a novel or play you would like to write. Your description should be interesting enough to make someone else read the completed work.

The rubric made clear that the students were free to write poems, essays or stories in all cases, except when a question included a specific requirement, so that fiction retained its importance in our practice. This freedom to choose is striking, and fits with the explicit view that young people write better when they are interested in what they are writing about. Throughout there are signs of a desire to encourage writing in which the young people explored their first-hand experience, the question about part-time employment with its detailed advice being clearly aimed in that direction. There are invitations to more intimate reflection in *Left Alone* and the question concerned with actions that the writer is proud or ashamed of. Others topics too point in that direction, including *Reading character from clothes* and *Spring*. Even a title such as *A Foreign City* or *All Mod. Cons.* might lead to "personal writing", as we called it. This selection of topics, though made for the specific purposes of an examination, precisely characterises two important strands in our teaching: it was not just that we were encouraging pupils to write about their lives, but we were even moving fictional writing closer to first-hand experience. The presence of a poem by Larkin is itself significant; these were the years of "kitchen sink" novels and verse, which themselves offered a carefully edited version of the lives of ordinary people.

I have already made clear in the section about the fifth form that by the early sixties there had been radical changes in the nature and purpose of the teaching of writing, and these were certainly not confined to the Minchenden department or even to LATE. The idea that it was best to learn to write by first practising with sentences, then with paragraphs and then with whole essays had long disappeared. We had become convinced that the writing of exercises about neutral topics of little or no interest to our pupils was counter-productive, and that they would best develop their existing language competences through writing that engaged their interest. The struggle to say something that mattered would challenge them in a way that mere exercises could not be expected to. We didn't wish their "interests" merely to be fashionable topics for the young: popular music, for example, was associated via specialist magazines with a highly artificial style that we thought would constrict rather than develop their abilities. Our unconscious models were the prose and verse of contemporary provincial writers, such as those described as *kitchen sink,* who had used their writing as means of interpreting their own milieux and of taking up an attitude to their lives as a way making roles for themselves in them. Beyond these the overall influence of the young D.H.Lawrence could be detected. Our own education was of course highly significant here, for most English teachers too in our years of adolescence and young adulthood had found writing prose or verse in an intimate manner about some aspects of our lives helped us in various ways. The underlying qualities we valued were truth to experience, but it was a limited kind of experience. Person to person relationships, especially within the family and between the sexes, played a central role in the kind of writing we valued; it was not until later that we began to look beyond the interpersonal to wider themes. It is interesting to notice that our pupils themselves were to an extent subverting our intentions since many of them preferred to write fiction than to face the demands of reinterpreting their own worlds. Some of them, no doubt, would not have wished to make available some aspects of their lives, and so created acceptable substitutes on the basis of clues gathered from the stories and poems we read together.

There were several influences moving English teaching in this direction. A book, *The Excitement of Writing,* by Alex Clegg, the Director of Education for the West Riding of Yorkshire, had been widely influential in encouraging writing close to first-hand experience and couched in quasi-literary modes. David Holbrook's quirky but energetic advocacy of *creative writing* in a series of books about English teaching must have had an effect too, for the books were much referred to. Almost equally influential – at least in London – was a series of competitions organised by *The Daily Mirror* newspaper to select outstanding writing, mainly in verse, written by school pupils, the results being published in a series of booklets. We in LATE were particularly aware of the competition because Harold Rosen was one of the committee of judges. At Minchenden my colleagues and I submitted our students' best work and a surprising number of pieces eventually appeared in the annual publications.

It would be a mistake to accept this policy of the sixties solely in the terms that we its advocates would have used. Sometimes the writing did indeed achieve an exploration of personal experience: *The Death of a Perch,* which was quoted in an earlier section, is a clear example. The extracts that follow are exceptional, chosen to show "personal" writing at its best. The first was written by a seventeen year old girl in the sixth form; writing of this kind was not required in the examination, which was entirely concerned with literary criticism. As the piece is long I shall quote only parts of several paragraphs.

A Perfect Moment

My sister had gone out and taken little Jackie to the park. "Keep an eye on Alison", she said. Alison's just a few months old and never cries so I was quite happy to keep an eye on her. I was reading *Mansfield Park* – I found I was enjoying rereading it – and then Alison started crying. She'll only go to sleep again in a moment, I thought...

But then she was crying again and so *Mansfield Park* was put down and I carried her into the sitting room. She was warm and fat and soft, and I held her very close and she sat right back in the crook of my arm. She smelt warm and milky and the pulse on the top of her head made the brown hairs beat up and down...

Then I called her name and she looked right at me, and her eyes were suddenly big and serious and really intelligent, and I chatted to her, the baby words coming out in a tone ridiculously sweet and exaggerated, and she smiled, a really happy intelligent smile, and I said something that we both knew was funny and we smiled at each other, and she laughed – just a little chuckle ...

She was going to be terribly clever ... I'll take her out to London, to all the interesting places and I'll buy her beautiful books and clothes, and she'll never feel the kind of indifference that I feel about my aunts ...

Then my sister came home and I left Alison with her and then I knew that in a few years' time I'll probably be married and have my own children and we'll mean very little to each other...

I valued this not only for its openness about an intimate experience but also for more literary virtues, such as the precision of observation of the pulse on the head, and the way in which the experience for all its warmth is carefully moved to a distance at the end, the writer acknowledging to herself as well as to the reader the elements of self-deception in the experience.

Although the examination that the sixth form students were being prepared for was solely concerned with English Literature, it was departmental policy to see to it that the writing they did was not only literary criticism, which we felt to be too restricted a genre to constitute an adequate education on its own. Not all of the writing was so intimately personal as *A Perfect Moment*; here is an untitled poem by a seventeen or eighteen year old girl:

The rain drips with primitive persistence,
Bouncing off my trowel, and splashing
On to the slab of bed-rock at my feet.
I watch the hostile mud

Obliterating for ever the subtle distinction
Between layer 6 (chocolate brown humus)
And layer 7 (brown clayey soil
With fragments of stone).
Above my bedraggled turf-line I see
Huddling groups seeking the meagre comfort
Of thermos tea; a tired shoveller
Indulging in the unwonted luxury of a long stretch;
The Director in vehement discussion
About the merits of timber-laced ramparts,
Pointing emphatically with his trowel –
A gesture that conveys all archaeology.

And suddenly I am aware of the largeness of life –
Not the largeness that the mountains and the stars show,
Those silent judges of our insignificance –
But the sheer size of human experience,
That long progression that links me with the Iron Age,
And justifies my trench-bound presence in prehistory.

Of course, not many sixth form pupils could write with this level of skill and sophistication. I have chosen this piece because it displays another kind of engagement with first hand experience. I value it not so much because of the realistic details of the dig, but for the attempt to come to grips with much more difficult feelings. I quote this and the previous example to show that our claim to be helping young people to realise who they were and where they were going was not entirely unreasonable. (I believe that this writer did indeed become an archaeologist of some distinction.) Against occasional pieces like these, however, must be placed the much greater number of highly skilful pieces that simulated personal exploration but were in fact constructions that owed more to the literature that was being read than to the writers' engagement with experience. The distinction I am making is a crude one, since all writing is influenced by existing models, but at that time – perhaps wrongly – we valued more highly those pieces that clearly looked towards first-hand experience. The two writers whose pieces are quoted above had indeed taken care of a sister's baby and worked on an archaeological dig. Many other pieces that were skilfully wrought were not direct reflections of experienced events, as for example the outstanding poem *Uncle Died*, which I quoted in a previous section.

Here for example is a poem written by a third year girl which does not seem to have been developed from an actual event.

Nice Weather We're Having

It's strange:
What unimportant, dismally petty things
You think about. And talk about.

The last thing I ever said to him
Was, "Nice weather we're having".
He agreed. All the things
That could have been said
While I was 'passing time'.
But it's too late now.
And you think of what it might
Have been:- "I love you – remember
That always". Or "I'll always think of you".
Instead – "Nice weather we're having".
And he agreed.
Travelling in a car, like that,
You sometimes see an accident,
And you think, "My God,
It might have been us."
But it was.

When I awoke it was noisy.
People's voices wailing with fear –
A nameless sea of faces, contorted with compassion.
A child sucking a lollipop.
A pink lollipop.
Seemingly magnified out of all proportion.
Under one arm, hanging limply, a teddy bear,
One eye gone, and in its place
A grisly socket, showing the sawdust.
The other eye stared ceaselessly at me.
The eye seemed to have enormous depth
As I gazed into it,
Glinting and twinkling evilly in the sunlight,
A sunlight gone suddenly dull
With fear and bewilderment.
The thoughts going through my bursting brain:
"It's strange,
What unimportant, dismally petty things
We think about".
It began to rain.

This is exploration of experience, but it is imagined experience. By saying this I am not intending to devalue the poem. I find much to admire in this piece by a thirteen or fourteen year old: the everyday language that occasionally comes to a sharper focus, the collocation of triviality and tragedy, the sudden introduction of the road accident, the skilful turn about so that the end reflects the beginning. The handling of the teddy bear image may strike an adult reader as histrionic, but it is nevertheless remarkable for so young a writer. (To note that the image probably derives from the cinema is not to devalue it, for it has been very successfully transmuted into verse.) I certainly did not "teach" these skills: how could I have done? They were achieved through close attention to how adults write, and by ingenious experiment and inventiveness. Writing of the quality of the three I have quoted is of course exceptional. Nevertheless, even though it was produced by a highly able students, it stands as an important justification of the kind of teaching of writing that does not make the teaching of skills its primary task but provides a milieu which supports the pupils' experiments.

The emphasis upon personal and fictional writing was not the whole story, however. When I began teaching it was expected that able pupils by the time they left school should be able to write about topics of general interest, though these tended to be of the toothless kind such as: 'Is it better to Live in the Town or the Country?'. I had continued to require occasional writing about social and ethical matters when they arose during discussions, often provoked by works of literature that we had been reading. Even able pupils did not write so well about topics that required discussion and the marshalling of evidence, and it was far from clear how best to help them. I had long ago abandoned the practice of asking pupils to provide a plan of a piece of non-narrative writing before attempting to write it, for such plans proved usually to contain nothing but vague gestures such as "Give my opinion about X", and "Say why I think that". It seemed that planning was mainly useful to an experienced writer whose topic was already partly structured in his or her understanding. Even the oldest of my pupils needed first to find out what kind of things they were able to say before trying to put them into order, so that I found that preliminary discussion, and the writing of short paragraphs, followed by reordering of ideas at the blackboard was the most useful way of helping them to find some shape for their thoughts.

My last two or three years at Minchenden School, from 1963 to 1966, were characterised by an attempt to bring the work I was doing with my pupils closer to the kinds of reading, writing and talking that adults engage in during their lives. I became concerned about the heavy emphasis upon story telling that characterised some English curricula, partly because the version of English with literature at its centre seemed to have moved too far away from the everyday uses of English in our society. In about 1963 or 1964 Jimmy Britton gave a lecture in which he argued that English for older students should not confine itself to stories and autobiographical writing but should acknowledge that much of the writing that adults do is engaged with the real world, often with an attempt to change it in some way. This coincided with his presenting the distinction between *language in the role of participant* and *language in the role of observer* that later played an important part in his research. This was a change of emphasis in that LATE had previously urged that since most of the curriculum asked pupils for impersonal writing English ought to concentrate on more personal kinds. I can now see that this earlier stance was linked with the pre-eminence of literature in the English curriculum. If works of literature were central to the English curriculum, then it would be natural for the writing required of pupils to be itself literary, poems, stories and even plays. Even anecdotal and biographical writing would thus be banished to the periphery, unless they took a literary form. Though I later became uneasy at how Jimmy defined the difference between *observer* and *participant,* I gratefully welcomed the proposal of a balance between personal and public writing in the English curriculum, which was soon reflected in our school examinations for older students.

My rationale for wishing to minimise the distinction between personal and impersonal writing was that fifteen-year-old boys and girls are more than ready to look out into larger worlds and to commit themselves to a passionate interest in topics that may vary from the social to the scientific. The approach of a young person to these enthusiasms, however, may differ widely from the coolly analytical one favoured in many school subjects. In English lessons a topic could be explored in ways that enabled students to express their sense of its social or ethical importance, so that their feelings and commitment could be acknowledged. We believed that English should enable students to make the public issues their own. It was in this way that we justified the inclusion of a wider range of topics in English lessons, and opened the door to encouraging pupils to write about social and political issues. It seems that in the sixties we were moving further and further away from an English that was a precious possession of the few, and seeking to place the subject firmly in the lives we saw about us, and we were doing so with an unmistakable moral passion. Leavis's contention that English at best provides a *critical* training was being extended in order to encourage our students to take a critical perspective on the world they were experiencing, though he might not have approved the nature of this extension.

These moves towards the world outside school, however, led to a further change of emphasis. I wanted to get away from the artificiality of so much schooling, the setting of tasks that were no more than preparatory practice, many of them very distant from the real practices in everyday life that they were supposed to prepare students for. At that time this was particularly noticeable in the writing demands of English. Very few adults ever find themselves writing anything like an English essay of the kind required in examinations, except perhaps in other academic contexts, while the absurdity of the old *precis* still lingered in a few examination boards. Members of LATE were striving to find tasks for writing that would approach much nearer to the writing that adults – at least adults like ourselves – might engage in. Thirty or more years later, however, I am aware that only a restricted social group engages in the kinds of writing we had in mind, drafting a proposal, preparing a pamphlet, writing up an interview, and so on. However, that is not necessarily a criticism of our intentions, since we wanted to open up public writing to all of our pupils. We saw that the skills of writing for unknown audiences are necessary to anyone who was to take a full and active part in our society. It was for later decades to find out how restricted a range of reading and writing most adults do engage in, particularly at work.

It is not easy to identify precisely what provoked this shift in my teaching and that of other teachers. During those years of my teaching, profound changes in the English teaching were taking place in many other schools. Typical of the new emphases was the book *Reflections,* prepared by LATE members at Walworth School, but published and popularised across the country, which disseminated the idea that the English curriculum should be focused upon *themes* such as Parents and Children, The Neighbourhood, or Freedom and Authority. This was not very far from our own practice at Minchenden. The idea of the classroom conversation – and our awareness that it was our responsibility to make the talk pedagogically valuable – led us to introduce topics that would provide a focus for reading, talking and writing that was relevant to our pupils' lives, both their first hand experiences and the public events that they read and heard about. Of course, we cannot separate the emphases that made up the curriculum that was realised in our lessons from the wider culture about us. It was the time of the Cuban Crisis, and the years when the Campaign for Nuclear Disarmament was most strongly supported: the destruction of us all in a nuclear conflagration seemed an ever-present possibility. Helping young people to be aware of the socio-political world that they were growing up in seemed an important responsibility; we looked forward to a future in which most people in this country would be critically aware of the political and economic policies that impinged on their lives. We thought arrogantly that English was the most important subject in the curriculum precisely because it enabled us to approach value-laden topics closed to most other teachers. But it was also a time of relative economic expansion and prosperity, and this seems to have been related to the optimism felt by many liberal minded teachers about what education might do to improve the quality of life for our pupils. In LATE and elsewhere teachers were particularly concerned about doing their best for children from *disadvantaged homes:* it was the time of the Newsom Report and of an increasingly influential campaign for comprehensive schools that would offer secondary education to all. To understand our teaching of English all this must be taken into account. In spite of the awareness of danger, for many teachers it was a time of enthusiasm generated by hope.

The wish to relate the English curriculum to what was going on outside school was far from a wish to impose on pupils the requirements of commerce and industry. It was not until the eighties that schools began to consider seriously the relevance of curricula to the world of work, or to other aspects of adult life, and it was even later that the English curriculum became influenced by this line of thought. My own thoughts about English may have been influenced by meeting at the new National Association for the Teaching of English teachers such as Fred Flower who was principal of a college of further education. Since those years we have seen much more attention being given to non-literary forms of writing, but many English teachers even now in the nineties look suspiciously at it, as a strategy to make the purposes of schooling subservient to those of employers. The tension between these two value systems – English as a vehicle for intrinsic values or as relevant to daily life – continues today; perhaps some of today's English teaching is as much shaped by unexamined literary preconceptions as mine was for many years. In the early sixties, many members of LATE were clear that they wanted to arm their pupils to be active and critical participants in adult life.

I had intended to represent the impersonal and public writing by quoting questions that formed part of an examination paper that was intended to contrast with the paper (quoted above) that was focused on personal and fictional writing, but when I examined them they were different from what I had expected. It seemed as if my colleagues and I had not moved so far in that direction as we thought, for many of the tasks were little different from those set in the *personal writing* examination. For example:

- If you had as much money as you liked to spend on clothes what would you buy? (Remember you would need different clothes for different occasions.)

Two new elements do appear, however. There are questions requiring letters:-

- You have been given the address of an English family who live in France and who, you hear, may want holiday help with their house and three children. Write a letter offering your services for six weeks during this summer. Your success depends upon the impression given by your letter.
- Imagine that you are a pupil at an old, run-down and badly equipped school, and that you have been chosen by your classmates to write a letter to the governors about these conditions; this is an unorthodox action and you try to temper its boldness with a tone of respect; not an easy thing to do because you feel strongly about the conditions and describe them very bluntly.

These letters represent a change of emphasis by laying down conditions to which the writing had to conform, by outlining an imaginary situation, readership and purpose for the writing, though such artificial – and rather unconvincing – simulations had appeared in earlier textbooks. The rubric gave some emphasis to the style in which the letters were to be couched, and this throws light on our teaching at this time, which was directed towards *appropriateness* of writing to a particular context and purpose, rather than an overall concept of *good English*, which we had concluded to be unreal and misleading. The second new element that appeared in this set of questions was that we explicitly invited our pupils to write about social and political issues, for example:

- You are thinking of selling your house. Your neighbour, with whom you are quite friendly, comes to ask you not to sell it to a coloured person. Write this either as a play or a narrative. Try to avoid rudeness.

The writing that this examination paper gave rise to was not very different from that elicited by the "personal writing" paper; some of the questions – especially the piece related to ethnic prejudice – drew from our pupils pieces of writing not different in kind or quality from the best answers to the other paper. These examination tasks do not seem to approximate closely to the *impersonal* writing tasks that I set up in lessons, so it is to my memories of teaching that I must turn in order to represent them.

I can recollect several lessons shaped by the desire to bring work in English closer to the uses of language in adult life. With a fourth form I had become engaged in a discussion of work and the choice of a career. This was a realistic topic for boys and girls who would win qualifications and probably go on to college and university. Most of them knew about the kinds of employment that members of their family were engaged in and were very interested to know about others. I therefore suggested that we should find out by interviewing relatives and friends. It was innovative to suggest that pupils might collect material to write about: no doubt the popularity of investigative sociology made this seem a possible method. This led to the devising of questions – probably through work in small groups, followed by class discussion – and trying them out, and to some teaching of interview techniques, though I made no claim to expertise. When, after discussion at the blackboard, a satisfactory format for all to use had been arrived at, each student carried out an interview. I suspect that most were interviews of mothers or fathers but the reports preserved anonymity. When the students came back with their notes on the interview – tape-recorders were not yet common – we discussed how to write them up, agreeing a common format. (I hope it was a discussion and not a diktat.). The notes were written up as a continuous account of the demands of a particular job, and the pleasures and problems of carrying it out. The resulting accounts were first passed round the class and discussed informally, next read and responded to by me in the usual way, and then placed anonymously in a ring file and made available in their form room ("home room"). I had abandoned one of the central principles of the *Scrutiny* view of English, for the demands of work were held to be intrinsically inimical to the literary and cultural values on which Cambridge English was predicated, but I do not think that I was aware of this. I was reaching out towards a form of writing that was more than an exercise to satisfy a teacher, and that had some real function in the community, even if only that of the school. Of course, so long afterwards I cannot know how valuable it was to them in developing new language skills, but it well illustrates how the desire to link the curriculum with life outside school influenced my work at that time.

Out of the blue comes another memory from this time. As the school had been increasing in size there had been talk about the building of a further block of classrooms and laboratories, so I used this as the basis for some work with a fourth year class. They worked in groups of perhaps four or five pupils, and had the task of agreeing a plan of the building and justifying what they included. Many years later I learnt that to carry out a project of this kind an architect would first set out to study the context, the perceived requirements of users, and the financial constraints, but the task as I then conceived it was not sophisticated enough to require my pupils to investigate these matters.

Each group eventually reported first orally to the class, dealing with questions and criticisms, and then in diagrams and writing in the form of a display that to be fastened on the wall of the classroom. I had taken a step towards real life tasks, and included spoken language in the outcome. In the light of later developments in oracy it was not a major advance, but it was highly significant for me at a time when even those few teachers who accepted some responsibility for developing their pupils' spoken language had no clear conception of purpose and methods.

I had accepted a new direction of development and often used a similar pattern of work during my last few years at Minchenden, but I had no conception of where this might lead. Work done in groups found its culmination in oral reports to the class as a whole, followed by discussion in which I was able to underline certain matters, propose qualifications and generally manage the emphases. I did my best to ensure that my commentary did not amount to a rejection of what the group had done. Each group would also have prepared a wall-display containing texts and relevant visual material, such as diagrams. (An attempt to include drawings and other graphics was a failure because of the poor quality of what was done and my inability to offer help of the kind needed.)

My third example comes, I think, from work with a third form during those years. The discussion in the lesson had moved towards the experience of being a new boy or girl in the school. I do not know how the topic arose: perhaps I had been asking them to write about their first days at the school. Some members of the class said that their first few days would have been more comfortable if they had been given more information and advice about the school and the requirements it placed upon its most junior members. I did not know whether this was a reasonable observation but it became the cue for a writing task. Unfortunately at that point my memory fails, though Dorothy reminds me that some – or all? – of the students visited the top class of a primary school and talked to the eleven year olds about their expectations and fears for their first days at a secondary school. I imagine that after this visit my students worked in groups deciding what information to include, and then produced drafts based on this. I do not know whether each pupil wrote an individual version of the group's list of information, or whether each group collaborated in producing one draft. Nor do I know what was done with the accounts: I would expect that they were offered to the primary school children and perhaps to first years pupils for their comments and – could one hope? – their use.

Along with other members of LATE I had at this time begun to acknowledge an important principle in setting written work, that part of our task as teachers was to ensure that we were supplying students with all the information they needed to write appropriately. When we write a letter we usually know or can imagine whom we are addressing, at least well enough to judge what is relevant and what style is appropriate. The journalist has quite precise ideas about the readership of a particular journal, and most novelists are working within a genre that helps them to make crucial choices. But who is the school pupil writing for? In one sense the audience is the teacher, but the teacher not as an individual but as representative of a set of educational expectations, though not all pupils will have equal access to these expectations unless the teacher makes it his or her business to make them available. Our contention was that these expectations should be made as explicit as possible whenever work was set; the "nature of the task and audience" should be "specified", I wrote. This important principle had been much discussed in LATE, and a few years later the concept of "audience" was to play a central role in several projects investigating writing in schools to be carried out by James Britton, Nancy Martin, Harold Rosen and others. My next two examples illustrate how I tried to carry this out.

With fifth form students too, in spite of examination requirements, I looked more and more to find activities, particularly for writing, that were closer to adults' uses of language. One piece of work arose from some talk about emigration, a topic that attracted some of the class. I had come across an article in *The Listener* about the status of women in Australia so I read it to my fifth year class, simplifying and abridging it. After some discussion I told them to pretend to be clerks in the immigration department at Australia House, and to use the material from the article in writing a letter in reply to one from a woman who was considering emigrating to Australia. My purpose was not merely to simulate a task from one adult milieu amongst many but to set up a situation in which the content and style would be implicit in the task and the audience the writing was to be addressed to. I *hope* that I took the opportunity to discuss this with my students, rather than leaving them to intuit what these requirements would be. In retrospect I can see that it was not *just any kind* of adult language that I was interested in, but the language of those adults who are in a position of power. It was the language of power that I wanted to put at my pupils' disposal, though I may not have phrased it in that way to myself. It is worth noticing that the source of the topic was the classroom conversation, and not a work of literature.

Another piece of work could only have been attempted with *mixed classes* whom I knew to trust me. (The fifth year article provides me with details.) I put my students in the position of a copywriter for an advertising agency who is asked by his boss to write a pamphlet for mothers of one-year-old children. One of the agency's customers, a firm selling equipment for small children, proposed to advertise: 'Mothers! Have you a one-year-old child? Send for our pamphlet …' Their boss told them to write a pamphlet of genuine good advice but to mention – and illustrate – the firm's products incidentally. Some of the boys replied that they knew nothing about babies, so I said, 'That's exactly what you said to the boss, and all he did was to give you this book and tell you to find out.' I read to them the appropriate chapter from Dr Spock's *Baby and Child Care* – with, I must admit, some omissions. The students made a list of suitable products and noted some of the advice given to mothers. Most of the class took the task very seriously and produced pamphlet-like documents illustrated with pictures cut from magazines or drawn by themselves. In most cases the text showed how fully they had already internalised the language and mannerisms of advertising copywriters.

Even at that time I had to acknowledge the artificiality of the roles that I asked these adolescents to take on, though they seemed to enjoy the tasks. Such simulation is in fact very unlike writing for a real purpose that has arisen in one's own life. (I can now contrast this with the class in a TVEI project that was able to design a bridge for a dockyard, and then to see their proposed design actually built.) At that stage I did not see these tasks as *preparation for the world of work,* for that formulation was still twenty years away from schools, though no doubt it could have been found in Further Education. Rather the task was to give the students an experience of summarising and reusing material as we do in adult life, in the interests of specified purposes and for an identifiable audience. I saw exercises of this kind, for all their artificiality, as a considerable improvement on the traditional *précis,* with its unvarying demand for paraphrase to a third of the length, whatever the nature of the passage, and the stupid unawareness that when one selects material from a passage it is normally for a particular purpose and addressed to a particular audience.

10 Small Groups and Talk

Even when I began teaching in January 1950 I was aware that English teachers had some responsibility for spoken language. I knew that some teachers made much use of improvised drama but I don't think I saw that in relation to speech, but in a category of its own. As a pupil I had met the form-alised procedures of debate, with the roles of chairman, proposer and seconder and opposer and seconder, and I certainly made some use of discussion and debate from the very first. The headmaster at Carlton gave me the responsibility for organising meetings of a school debating society; I imagine that we set up uncontroversial controversies of the "Town versus country" and "corporal punishment" variety, which I found boring, though I remember that one of my older pupils proved to be a very skilled speaker. I believe that I may also have set up such *debates* with some classes, but I soon abandoned them in favour of informal discussion. The more I found matters of genuine interest to discuss with my pupils, the less I would think to set up talk for talk's sake. By the time I reached Minchenden such practices had long been forgotten, for a quite different kind of attention to spoken language had become necessary.

I can trace a sequence of events and changing perceptions during my latter years at Minchenden that led to a very significant shift of focus as more and more time in my lessons was given to group discussion. The coming of the tape-recorder into schools – I first made use of one in about 1961 or 1962 – did not immediately have a marked effect, but was to do so in time. At this time even LATE did not have a clear view of its uses. At first we saw it as an instrument for evaluating the spoken language of older students, but did not perceive the problems of validity. It did not immediately occur to us that one sample taken in a particular context might not validly represent the universe of different kinds of spoken behaviour. Not did we realise that how our pupils perceived the situation we put them in – what they thought we wanted from them – would greatly influence their behaviour and play a significant part in the scores. One member of LATE suggested that we could use the tape recorder to prepare programmes of poetry and other reading to play to our classes, and I did in fact do this at least once. The term "oracy" had not yet been invented, but our pupils' talk was beginning to take up an important place in the curriculum. I have already mentioned taking part in discussions of the English syllabus for the new CSE examination. The effort to persuade other teachers on the panel about the importance of talk made me reflect more consciously on the principles I was committed to. In all of the CSE panels there was much discussion of the case for and against the inclusion of a test of spoken language, and eventually the decision was made to include spoken language as a compulsory element and I believe that this applied to CSE examinations in all parts of the country. The General Certificate of Education too changed its policy and made it possible for schools to opt for their candidates for English Language to be set speech tests.

These changes in the public status of spoken language persuaded us in the Minchenden department to carry out during one year a mock oral test of the fifth year students, recording them in small groups and awarding scores to each individual and each group. We learnt a good deal about the difficulties of doing this, particularly the heavy demands on evaluators' time, but were also impressed by the high level of ability shown by most of our pupils. It seemed that, for many of them, discussion of serious topics with their peers when not directed by an adult released hidden strengths – of personality as well as of speech. Even though I had been using group talk for some years as one strategy available in teaching it was the recorded discussions of that year (probably 1964/5) that fully opened my eyes to the possibilities of talk for learning. I have a very clear memory of some of those early recordings, particularly a fifth year group discussing a contemporary poem called *Andromeda*. This group contained three girls and two boys, all about sixteen years of age and academically successful. The discussion was rather diffuse, which is not unusual, so in the interests of brevity I have made some omissions in quoting part of the opening sequence. The poem (by Graham Hough) uses the Andromeda legend to comment on the way some women have little choice but to accept domesticity and devote themselves to home making, however churlish and unappreciative their husbands are. This Andromeda looks after her unattractive "monster" and sweeps the cave, and seems remarkably unimpressed by the young "hero" who comes to save her. (In the transcript I indicated with (B) or (G) whether a boy or a girl was speaking.)

> (G) Who's the monster?
> (B) I couldn't find out.

Omission

> 7. (G) Why didn't they name the ...?
> 8. (G) Surely it's not the point of whether it's got a name or not.

Omission

(G) Why does it say she swept the dark sea from the door?

(G) Because it's so pointless being there ...

(G) I don't get this line: "Fretted at unsuccessful business deals".

(B) I don't know... It seems to be comparing it with a modern business man, or something. Yes, you know... sort of the wife chained to the ... kitchen sink..., you know.

(G) It says..."the next meal" ... sort of the pointlessness of the whole *life*, you know.

(G) Who is it being rescued by a handsome young whatsit? *[The text describes him as "the heaven-sprung hero".]*

Omission

(G) But she doesn't want to be rescued.

(B) No, it's not that she doesn't want to be rescued. The hero doesn't want to rescue her.

(GG) No, no, no.

(G) The first line: "One can get used to anything".

(G) She's quite resigned.

(B) Yes. Yes. But I mean the hero doesn't want to rescue her either.

Omission

(B) How do you work that out?

(G) "He had not come for this." He wasn't prepared for her being

...

Domesticated. *[Several voices.]*

(B) Oh, I see... Yes, you're right.

(G) Then he goes away because he realises that she doesn't *want* to be rescued.

(B) What's the point of the whole thing anyway?

Omission

(B) I don't think it's all about a myth, though, is it?

A few minutes later, after expressions of frustration and some rereading of the poem, one of the girls said:

But it's just like life... I mean you sweep the house out and the dirt comes back ... so you sweep it out again.

And they continued to work on the poem.

When I listened to this recording I was pleased by the group's progress in understanding the poem, and not at all surprised to find that it was the girls who made more sense of it. However, I was even more impressed by the way in which they approached it. Not only did they repeatedly return to the text looking for further evidence, but they collaborated effectively, asking for one another's interpretations, justifying assertions, persuading, and so on. They were supportive rather than competitive, and accepted correction and explanation from others. At that time even when teaching highly intelligent young people such as these we had not yet recognised the competence in collaborative talk that would make them able to work effectively without adult direction. For all its strengths, the *Andromeda* discussion now seems less impressive than some of the talk about poems that I recorded in later years. In 1964/5 it was the discussion of general issues that produced the most impressive talk in those groups. I remember in one of them a boy leading with some brilliance, showing the most sophisticated skills of *chairing* without their having been taught. Unfortunately I didn't transcribe any of those recordings.

What the tape recorder first led us to was an general interest in spoken language and its uses in school, since we could now record and play back the discussions that our pupils had in small groups during our lessons, which then focused our attention upon their contribution to learning. We were now able to listen reflectively to what was said, in a way impossible in the classroom itself with its urgent multiple demands on a teacher's attention. As a result we began to perceive quite differently what processes the talk was contributing to. At first my colleagues and I had been a little uncertain whether the skills of speaking and of managing interpersonal relationships should be at the centre of our attention, but later it became clear that talk was to be primarily important as a tool of learning, just as writing was. This was very significant for me and led to a greatly increased use of small group discussion during my last few years of teaching. Listening to pupils' talk, and finding unexpected value in it, gave a new perspective upon classroom talk as a whole, and certainly played its part in our appreciation of *the classroom conversation* as the basis for our teaching. Our emphasis upon talk changed the aspects of classroom learning that we valued and planned for, and thereby shifted the very nature of what we were offering to our students; changing the mode of communication in the classroom turned out to imply changing the curriculum.

Thus the coming of the tape recorder introduced what turned out to be radical changes in my teaching methods and those of my colleagues, and by the mid sixties the leading group in LATE, of whom I was now one, was not thinking primarily of talk as a skill in its own right but of talk as one means by which not only our pupils but all of us learn. The Plowden Report gave strong support to the primary teachers in LATE who already seemed to take it for granted that children's talk played a useful role in their learning. For all my increasing use of work in small groups I still believed that my management of lessons was central and essential, especially in leading discussions which involved the whole class, since this provided a frame of reference – and enabled re-emphasis of points – that increased the value of the small group talk. I accepted that, since the more intimate and exploratory talk happened more readily in small groups, much of the work would be done amidst a hum of small group conversation, which made the lessons very unlike those of an earlier generation of teachers who believed that work should be done in silence. At some point in the lesson I would usually ask groups to share what they had done with the rest of the class, or perhaps move them directly to individual reading and writing. I believed that the groups allowed a more intimate, hesitant, exploratory approach to a new topic, which could then be shared in the more organised and explicit terms demanded by the relatively public discussion in full class, itself the half-way stage to full explicitness in writing. Talking through a new set of ideas or tackling a problem together provided a means by which the students could work on their own thinking to modify and improve it. (It is interesting to notice that many of these phrases used at that time, such as "intimate, hesitant and exploratory" and "the full explicitness of writing", anticipated not only some of the central ideas that I later developed at Leeds, but even some of the words I was to use.) The sequence within the lesson matched the stages of a learner's journey into a new area of experience: the group discussion supported the class discussion, which in turn supported the writing.

The manner in which group discussion was integrated into work with the class as a whole proved to be crucial to its success. I must not underestimate the time that I spent in front of the class, presenting new topics or materials, raising questions to be investigated and discussed, moving the work of groups on to a new stage, managing the reporting back to the full class, questioning and encouraging critical reflection, or leading overall discussion of the topic, carefully underlining the main conclusions, and seeing to it that alternative views were represented. I had no doubt that all of these functions were crucial, but it seemed to me that they were far more effective when my pupils had already done work of their own to open up the issues. My own teaching was more effective when my students had already taken the measure of the topics we were dealing with. I wanted the talk in my lessons to be interactive; my students should be giving as well as receiving, so that the new understandings that arose would be as much theirs as mine. It was this reciprocal quality that we referred to when we chose the phrase *The classroom conversation*. I do not think it was entirely a figment of the imagination, but it would not have taken place without careful management.

Out of the changes in our attitude to the pupils' talking and writing came a conviction that when they did so they were working upon their views of how the world is, "talking for learning" as Jimmy Britton called it. In English lessons they were often dealing with the complexities of growing up, their sense of who they were, and their changing feelings about family and friends of the opposite sex, but we soon came to believe that their understanding of more substantive matters – social and moral issues for example – could also be changed through informal discussion. Jimmy Britton was again leading our thinking, but by now Harold Rosen was taking a major part too, and for Harold the release of working class pupils' abilities through valuing their speech was of prime importance. We had for some years seen that at best many of our pupils used their writing tasks as opportunity to reshape some aspects of their experience that they could produce in public. The writing clearly enabled them to review and reinterpret aspects of knowledge and feeling, and once we became fully embarked on encouraging extensive discussion in lessons it seemed that talk was having a similar effect.

One of the papers that survive from those years allows me to characterise my own part in these lessons. It seems that at the beginning of a lesson I provided a starting point by raising some issues. Next I outlined a task, often by writing it on the blackboard, and launched the groups on their work. Then I usually stood back for a while, just watching. It was not necessary to hear all that was said, for it was easy to see which groups had quickly found agreement and were trying out their idea, which were arguing eagerly, and which were frustrated or divided. Then I started walking round: groups that wanted help asked for it, the uncertain were spurred on by my audience, and where there were signs of social breakdown I could intervene and suggest solutions. I was careful not to push myself forward. At a certain stage in a group's work I had a role as temporary audience, to give enough approval to encourage the group to develop their ideas further. I had found that encouragement was sometimes more valuable than criticism, since advice from outside the situation often suggests moves not available to those inside. In thus describing my role in all group work at this time I may be underestimating my influence on what happened in the lessons, but this influence became less and less direct as I became more skilled using these methods. I believed that part of my task in these lessons was to serve as an assurance to the pupils that rational discussion and choice were possible. I remained the repository of standards, blocking the escape route labelled 'Anything Goes'. I was in no doubt about the importance of the teacher in group work, and at no time advocated a withdrawal from responsibility. On those infrequent occasions when it became clear that a class was not working seriously in small groups – perhaps because they found the topic unpersuasive or resented the lesson for another reason – I abandoned the group work immediately, and found some other approach. At no point did I think it proper to set a topic and abandon my pupils to their own devices.

Although during these last three or four years of classroom teaching I made much use of small group activities, I was always concerned to find a proper balance between the work done in small groups and that done by the undivided class, since the latter enabled me to guide and influence their understanding of what they were doing. I had no doubt that the teacher's role is crucial, for it is he or she who must set up the opportunities for learning, provide frameworks that will shape and direct it, and encourage reflective understanding of new experiences and ideas. When a class is working in small groups all the pupils can be actively involved; there need be no-one daydreaming at the back of the room. Each group can first try something out and then talk it over, all of the pupils being involved in the discussion and the effort to improve. Against this manifest advantage of group work we must place the fact that in full class discussion the teacher can lend to the class his own sense of purpose and his critical sense – that is, his sense of appropriate criteria and standards of judgement. My own practice was based on the assumption that pupils need both to borrow from the teacher and to have the opportunity to think and solve problems for themselves, so I aimed at a balance between work in full class and in smaller groups.

Work in groups can be regarded either as preparation for a presentation to the whole class or as an end in itself. I took the view that pupils fail to benefit from group work only if they are given a task that they cannot take seriously or if they are faced with failure. It must have been in about 1964 that we became aware of Vygotsky's work, which gave powerful theoretical support to the idea that putting our thoughts into words enables us to change our thinking, whereas Piaget had argued that language *follows* cognitive development, and thus cannot directly forward it. In my writings about talk at that time there was little sign of Vygotsky, though I had certainly read him with some care by then. If I had been asked at the time why group work had become so important for me I would have replied that it produced better work from pupils, not only in drama but throughout the English curriculum. The pragmatic rather than theoretical stance I adopted showed that I was still a teacher addressing myself to teachers. Perhaps, though, this underrates the influence of LATE theories, which not only persuaded me to try new methods but provided me with a rationale for them. I saw the work as useful because I had learnt to perceive it so.

Reports of LATE meetings held in 1963-66 show them still much concerned with the teaching of literature, though issues related specifically to pupils from working class backgrounds had come to the fore, linked inevitably with those who were not succeeding in school. At an evening meeting entitled "Custodians of Culture" the members present made it clear that in their view the task of English teachers did not include handing on high culture to the next generation. Much of the discussion was concerned with the divide between an English teacher's taste (for *Wuthering Heights,* perhaps) and that of pupils who were enjoying *Beach Party* or the novels of Ian Fleming. There was general agreement that the latter tastes did not represent a kind of corruption, since the pupils' response to those works included the ability to talk and write creatively. Thus we had detached ourselves from the Cambridge view that sensibility to literature was equivalent to ethical sensitivity, and justified this by the argument that crude self-assertiveness of the kind celebrated in Fleming's novels appears in *King Lear* too in the person of Edmund, but there it is expressed within an evaluative frame. We argued that it was the business of the classroom to provide the frame for our pupils' reading of the less acceptable literature. However thin this argument may now seem, it must have made some sense to me then as I wrote the report on the meeting, from which this paragraph is paraphrased.

LATE now sent us in another direction, and that probably reflected new interests of Jimmy Britton's. Some years before, many of us had rejected the traditional forms of grammar which were being taught in many schools. We argued that these ways of analysing language – clause analysis and parsing – were of little or no use to our pupils in improving their use of language, either in helping them to conform to standard usage or in encouraging them to use a wider range of more complex forms. We pointed out that the traditional systems had been developed during earlier centuries to describe the Latin language, and that they did not well match English, a very different non-inflected language. Not only did the systems omit many of the important characteristics of English, but many of the definitions to be found in text-books were nonsensical. For example, "A verb refers to a state or action" is not helpful since the very words "state" and "action" are clearly not verbs but nouns. But were there alternatives? At one meeting Michael Halliday explained his *scale and category* system of grammatical analysis, and this was followed by Pat Creek, a teacher member of LATE, talking about some lessons she had taught using contemporary forms of language study to help her secondary pupils understand how language works. I don't think I ever imitated her examples, but I did read the book by C.C. Fries that she recom-mended, and adapted some of the ideas in it for use with a fourth year form. Fries had an amusing way of using nonsense syllables to illustrate the differ-ence between *content* words and *structural* words. For example, we under-stand "An uggle wogs diggles" to mean that one thing carries out an action upon other things, even though the content words are nonsensical, since we use word order and *structural* words such as *An* to arrive at a hypothetical meaning. My fourth form found examples like this interesting but when I tried to move on further into Fries's structural analyses they found them incompre-hensible, even more, I fear, than the misleading definitions of *Latinate grammar,* as we scornfully called it. I also read some of the published work of Halliday whom I was later to meet and be influenced by, but not in my teaching in school. It seemed that the attempt to find alternative grammars that might be more useful to our pupils was doomed to failure.

I do not want it to seem that my teaching reflected the caricature of English teaching promulgated in the last two decades by the right wing press. I was concerned that my pupils should conform to normal practice in spelling and punctuation, and that when it was appropriate they should use the forms and structures normal in standard written English. Throughout my teaching I meticulously indicated errors and inappropriate expressions in the texts handed to me. At first I used to require pupils to copy out correctly those parts of the text that required correction, but after a year or two I decided that this was ineffective and discontinued it. I sometimes drew the attention of a class to common errors, and spent time with individual boys and girls who had particular problems with spelling and punctuation. It was not that my genera-tion of teachers didn't think spelling and punctuation important but rather that we decided that the methods used by our own teachers had been ineffec-tive. When I began teaching it was usual to give to pupils a variety of language exercises, including for example lists of sentences containing common sole-cisms in usage, such as a plural subject followed by a verb in the singular, which were to be corrected. However, like many other teachers during the fifties I came to believe that these exercises did little to eradicate the errors pupils made when writing, and my appreciation of the exercises was not enhanced by the fact that they often included pseudo-solecisms such as the final preposition and the split infinitive. I was more eager to persuade pupils to read carefully what they had written. As the years passed I thought it more important to respond to the content of what was written than to correct superficial errors, though I continued to do so. This was in line with our intention to engage young people in writing about matters that concerned them in their lives: as I used to say to my colleagues, who would tell a friend about their concerns if their friend corrected their grammar before responding to what they said?

I think that it was Harold Rosen who first realised that in the long run LATE's emphasis upon children's first-hand experience would produce a confrontation between a literature that on the whole was based upon middle class experience, and the very diverse language and experience of the majority of children. In the event it was the coming of *oracy* in the early sixties that forced the confrontation, since the awareness of pronunciation differences, the gap between *standard English* and class idioms, and finally differences in the perspectives with which life was approached by many young people compelled teachers to reconsider their values and emphases. In March 1965 Fred Flower, principal of a London College of Further Education, spoke at an LATE meeting about the Newsom Report on the education of pupils of secondary age. The Newsom Committee had taken the view that there was a great wastage of talent in the education of less academically successful pupils, so that the Report was largely concerned with reorganising the curriculum for fourteen year olds to bring it closer to their lives, and this acted to reinforce the direction that LATE had already taken in English. It was also very significant that, as Fred Flower pointed out, the then Secretary of State for Education, Edward Boyle, had committed himself in the Introduction to the view that it was possible for pupils to "acquire intelligence". This was a blow for the commonplace *wisdom* on which teachers had been reared, that intelligence was measurable, innate and unchanging. Boyle's courageous stand brought a breath of optimism to teaching.

The impact of social class upon children's ability to profit from schooling was very much in our minds during the middle sixties. At one LATE meeting, Basil Bernstein talked about his hypothesis that working class children were more likely to be limited to what he called "restricted codes" of language use, whereas much schooling depended upon "elaborated codes" characterised by high levels of explicitness, and Dorothy and I then took the trouble to read some of his early publications. At that time I was greatly interested in his theory, though later I came to think it misleading. Cultural differences between the language uses of social groups do indeed exist, and may have considerable influence upon children's education, but to translate them into just two rigid codes that constrained their future intellectual processes proved not to be enlightening. Since I was mainly concerned with more able pupils Bernstein's hypothesis had few implications for my teaching, except that it went to support my shift towards talk and writing directed towards explanation, planning, argument, and explicit rational analysis in general. My use of the blackboard to write down ideas proposed by members of the class seemed still more important in the light of Bernstein's ideas, since it provided a way of helping students of various ages to see how it is possible to reflect on what they were trying to say, and to look for possible structures in it.

Part of the move towards the world outside school was an interest in other media of communication besides written texts. It became acceptable to have older students examine newspapers and other popular publications with the critical intention of finding out how the genres worked. I attempted this with several third and fourth year classes, though not at a very sophisticated level, in comparison with the approaches that later became popular. In the early sixties, however, at Minchenden we were still partly in the grip of the devaluing perspective that came from Cambridge and the *Scrutiny* group; when we compared newspapers with one another, it was partly to direct the pupils' attention to misleading reportage, the manipulation of readers' feelings, and the trivialisation of news. I attended an LATE meeting at which Douglas Lowndes, who taught in a college of further education, spoke about the device he was using to encourage less able students of near adult age to write about their environment. He sent them out with cameras that provided instant pictures and instructions to photograph whatever interested them in the city streets around the college, for he had found that with their own photographs in front of them they were able to write in an engaged way about the life of the area, and their own attitudes to it. I have already mentioned the "radio ballads" Charles Parker had put together for the BBC; these represented an implicit shift of perspective. The "ballads" were documentary programmes made up of snippets of the recorded speech of working people, coal miners or deep sea fishermen, for example, talking about their lives without the intrusion of a *voice over* to reinterpret what speakers say. Edited together with suitable music written in a *folk song* style, they implicitly place a high valuation of people's lives and their speech. I tried with the help of a group of sixth formers to make a radio ballad about the school but we found the technical problems of editing the tapes too much for us. I was aware that other teachers were making innovative use of film with their students but I did not have a camera available and lacked the necessary skills. Teachers in comprehensive schools could hardly be unaware of the dominant part that television programmes were beginning to play in the everyday culture of their pupils, but the shadow of Cambridge still made me suspicious of its influence, so it was not until 1964 that Dorothy and I bought a set for our household. This was in spite of the fact that I was aware that other members of LATE, such as John Dixon, took a positive and even enthusiastic view of the possibilities of television. As it turned out in the decades that followed, the study of the media, including popular literature, song lyrics, television, and film, was to play a larger part in the English curriculum in many schools. What was different was that these popular media were looked at more sympathetically, since their success threw light upon the aspirations and dreams of millions of people. The further uniting of literature with life exemplified in *Women's Studies* and *Black Studies* was still far off, however.

The next step after accepting that talk as well as writing was an important tool of learning since it enabled pupils to review and reinterpret aspects of their knowledge and feeling, was to see this as more generally true, true *across the curriculum,* in the phrase invented by members of LATE for this purpose. If talk was valuable in English for developing understanding of the personal and social issues that was providing our subject matter, would it not be true for all subjects of the curriculum? If teachers of other subjects understood this it would improve the effectiveness of learning in other subjects. If only we could persuade teachers of science, history and so on to encourage pupils to talk and write about their work in an exploratory way, it would help them so make sense of new ideas. When I reread the fifth form paper I was fascinated to find in it many of the ideas – such as *exploratory* and *public* uses of language – that were eventually to inform my research. After I had left the classroom this line of thought led me to make an important distinction between *exploratory* and *presentational* talk, and the different roles they play in learning. It is clear that my experience and reflection as a practising teacher – not to mention my discussions with other members of LATE – laid down the basis for the work I did as an academic.

More immediately, the conferences organised by Harold Rosen for LATE in 1966 and 1968 and held at Beatrice Webb House were devoted to developing our understanding of how spoken language contributed to learning and to formulating policies for language in the classroom intended to influence all the teaching in a school. These moves in LATE eventually led to *Language, the Learner and the School* and the *language across the curriculum* movement, and in time profoundly influenced the Bullock Report. The formulation of questions about the function of spoken language in learning was indeed fateful for the direction of my life over the following thirty years, since after my move to the University of Leeds it led to my research into classroom language

In 1964 LATE asked me to convene a working party on the teaching of poetry, though my own preference would have been for a group to select another book of short stories. In the event it proved a very successful learning experience for most members, including me. Interesting people joined the group, including Peter Doughty, David McKay and other members of Michael Halliday's Schools Council development project, working at linguistics in the hope of clarifying its relevance for English teaching. There was also Robert Druce who had already published a book on poetry teaching, and several young teachers, including Tony Burgess and Dennis Brook, who were later to make names for themselves in the English field. It was an interesting group, and during the following two years we set ourselves the task of writing a book on the teaching of poetry. We took the underlying thesis that poetry should provide some of the voices in a "classroom conversation" that should include the voices of the pupils as well as the teacher. We undertook to write a chapter each, discussed what should be in it, the linguistics group providing some valuable underlying theory about the discussion of poetry, and then wrote drafts, which we brought back to the group for consideration. The book was completed but for all its virtues turned out not to be publishable; I still have a warm and appreciative letter written by Edward Boyle, by then working for Penguin Books, regretting that they could not publish it. Probably too many of us were inexperienced in writing for publication. (I have often wondered whether the typescript still exists somewhere.) For my own part, however, the thinking that took place in the poetry group played a valuable part in the shaping of later papers that I was to write. Indeed, other members of the group have said to me that for them too it was a seminal experience.

Some virtues of my methods of teaching literature showed themselves in a strange context in 1965 when I was invited to carry out a demonstration to a conference of the Joint Association for Classics Teaching. The organisers had apparently heard of "practical criticism", a phrase that encapsulated the approach to reading texts that was associated with Leavis and the Cambridge School of literary criticism, with its emphasis upon attention to the detailed texture of verse and prose, and they wanted to see how this could be carried out in a lesson. A Cambridge academic, Donald Davie, was invited the same day to make a demonstration of "practical criticism" with a group of his undergraduates. I took with me a group of upper sixth form students and gave them to read *The Quaker Graveyard in Nantucket*, an early poem by the American poet Robert Lowell; I thought that the very considerable difficulty in interpreting the details of the text would provide a partial parallel to the textual difficulty of reading literature in Latin or Greek. With a minimum of guidance from me the students set out with remarkable success to penetrate the poem, which they had never seen before. They did so well that they impressed even me. Whether it influenced any teachers of the classics is another matter.

It is hard to estimate the effect of the increasing visibility on my teaching during the years from 1959 to 1966, as the London Institute of Education sent more and more students to observe my teaching, from groups who came with a tutor – Frank Whitehead for example – and individual overseas educators, some of them senior in their own countries. I was also invited more and more often to lecture or write about my work. I became chair of LATE, and then its representative in the group that set up the National Association for the Teaching of English. It was in 1963 that I was nominated by NATE to be a member of the English Committee of The Schools Council for Examinations and the Curriculum, which was receiving national and local funding to carry out development throughout the curriculum. In 1965 I was a member of the group from NATE that set about planning in conjunction with the American National Council for the Teaching of English the international conference that was to become known as *The Dartmouth Seminar*. One undoubted effect was that I began to read books and papers about teaching that were recommended by the lecturers at the London Institute of Education and to take a more delib- erately theoretical view of what I was doing, almost as if I were preparing myself for an academic role. Neither my enthusiasm for LATE nor the later involvement in setting up NATE and the consequent taste of activities at national level were driven by ambition or by a sense that I would one day be an academic. Of course, I felt very flattered when my work was taken seriously and my opinions courted; my confidence increased greatly. Mostly, however, I was caught up in the excitement of new practices, and then in unwrapping the principles implicit in those practices. Later my part in the development not only of the NATE organisation but also of policies relevant to the educational/political issues that faced English teaching at that time created its own dynamic: I felt to be an actor in a movement that would change English teaching permanently and for the better. As a result I became far more widely aware of what was going on around me, instead of taking the political and cultural environment of teaching as inevitable and unchangeable. It is difficult to estimate how far all this influenced my teaching.

LATE also gave me an introduction to qualitative research, though that is not what I would have called it then. LATE working groups frequently took a topic and collected informal evidence to investigate it. For example one working party recorded small groups of pupils discussing poems and looked in detail at the discussions in order to find out what was happening, just as my colleagues and I at Minchenden did. These working parties led LATE members to an orientation to inquiry. The working parties did not claim to be doing research, but in effect they were, though of a distinctly informal kind. However, this provided the model that shaped a very significant part of my work when at Leeds I had groups of teachers to work with.

More than thirty years have passed since I ceased to be a school teacher, so that it is no surprise to find that my views of English teaching have changed in various ways. In this section I propose to discuss those changes as honestly as I am able.

TEACHING WRITING

At Minchenden School during the sixties my colleagues and I tried to make the values on which our approach rested available to all pupils. As I have explained, much of my "teaching" of writing amounted to presenting to my pupils implicit indications of what kinds of writing would be valued. This was achieved by sharing appropriate poems, plays and stories, and spending much time in discussing them and in improvised drama. At the same time, discussion of related topics persuaded pupils that their ideas and experiences were valid and acceptable, and that they had much to give in their writing. For all the successes of this approach to writing – and I have illustrated some of the best pieces above – I now judge that the contrasting methods I was using at Ruabon gave kinds of support to pupils' writing that were missing at Minchenden. During the Minchenden years I was successful in communicating what kinds of writing I valued, yet I wonder now whether I could have given my less adept pupils more help in learning how to write in the ways I was recommending. I would not want to abandon teaching writing in the way I did at Minchenden, but there are additional methods that now seem at least as valid and more supportive for many students, particularly some of the less able ones.

Some of the methods I was using at Ruabon deserved to be retained, for example the way in which I used the blackboard to show the students how to organise an essay. During recent years there has been discussion amongst educational theorists of the importance in learning of "metacognition", the ability to reflect upon one's own thought processes. Now this is a powerful intellectual tool that is almost universally relevant throughout our lives and especially an important element in the ability to write on impersonal topics, though not so important in narrative writing. To help a class prepare for writing I began by inviting them to make suggestions, and writing each suggestion somewhere on the blackboard. I tried to arrange the ideas in groups, and then to suggest relationships between them by various graphic devices, such as brackets, arrows, double-arrows, circles, underlining, and others. Later I asked my pupils to suggest interrelationships instead of supplying them myself, and began adding phrases describing relationships because the symbols proved too limited to express all the links that were needed. In this process I was in effect inventing strategies for representing relationships between ideas – metacognitive relationships – in order to help my students reflect on the structuring of their ideas before they committed themselves to writing. The strategies varied because the pattern required varied with the topic.

If we turn aside from the myth of poems and novels as spontaneous outpourings of perception and feeling – for they are seldom that – it is possible to focus the teaching of writing upon the idea of *craftsmanship*, though that was not a term we used in the sixties. The development of a craftsmanlike approach in young people necessitates alternative emphases and practices, amongst which I would number the kind of preplanning at the blackboard which I have already described and the writing of short paragraphs as a way of exploring possibilities and then discussing them. They would also include looking at the detailed textures and meanings of both adult writing and that done by the pupils themselves, in the manner that I used at Ruabon. With younger children especially this can be carried out through language games that help them become more sensitive to the language they are themselves using. The most difficult problem of teaching writing is that help needs to be offered not before or after but precisely at the time of drafting. Since I left school teaching there have been a number of techniques suggested to do this, such as *conferencing* which implied *redrafting*. In "conferencing", once a first draft has been attempted a series of consultations and discussions with other students and with the teacher is organised so that composition becomes a collaborative process, borrowing others' eyes to see more clearly what one has written, and what other possibilities remain.

There may however be a limit to the usefulness to students of this kind of help, for in Arts subjects there must always be areas of understanding and value that cannot be made fully explicit in a form that all pupils will be able to use. In helping students to structure an essay, it is possible to spend many lessons in illustrating how adult writers have shaped their work, and in taking the class through the processes on a blackboard, and yet find that some pupils have learnt little or nothing from the demonstrations. There is a wide gap between seeing how someone else shapes their ideas and using this to shape one's own thinking and writing.

The version of writing that was being promulgated in the sixties not only by LATE but also by those teachers influenced by Leavis and his collaborators was, as I have shown, primarily personal and literary. The two perspectives united in the new National Association for the Teaching of English (NATE), which in the later sixties and early seventies was able to speak with a very influential voice about what constituted English. I found – and I still believe – that most students, both more and less able, were very happy to write in a personal way about experience, to tell stories that reflected a version of life as they saw it (or as current writers told them to see it), or to compose poems that engaged with some aspect of contemporary experience, private or public. In the sixties many English teachers were enthusiastic about "personal writing" because it appeared to offer special opportunities to working class pupils who were ill at ease with impersonal forms of prose but could blossom when given the opportunity to tell stories. Perhaps we were too ready to accept stories, which may at times have become a way of avoiding more challenging forms of composition. However, not all students, even the most able ones, were at ease in personal writing. At the end of one of my last years in the school a girl came to tell me that she was not going to choose English in the sixth form. I was surprised by this because she had throughout the year produced the best written work in that fifth form, writing acutely observed and powerfully expressed poems and essays that explored her and others' experiences very openly. She chose to study modern languages and I was horrified when she explained she had hated doing the written tasks I had set during the fifth form year. It was clear that writing about her own experiences had made her feel vulnerable. Where had I gone wrong? I had certainly lavished praise on her, perhaps making her success too much a public performance. I suspect that if she had been writing for her own purposes and for an audience of friends rather than for evaluation she would have enjoyed exercising her considerable skill. It may be impossible to choose a version of the English curriculum (including a style of English teaching) that is going to suit the needs of every student.

My generation of English teachers often saw themselves as *freeing* children to write, as if it were possible to write or even talk without responding profoundly to what others have already said and written as well as to others' expectations which necessarily influence everything we say or do. We ignored the pressure of models and genres, and even underrated the influence upon our pupils of the models and priorities that each of us presented. Perhaps we were trapped by the assumptions of twentieth century Late Romanticism, in which D H Lawrence and his lesser followers used poems and novels as a way of elaborating versions of their private experiences. It is worth asking whether everyone should use writing to search for meanings in first-hand experience. Need literature always be individualistic or (at worst) solipsistic? Are not other forms of writing equally valid? Our unacknowledged model for all communication was (I think) the lyrical poem, seen as if it existed as a purely private creation, though poems too respond tacitly to what has been written before, or at least to how it has been written. I wonder now whether our belief that writing changes the self, that our pupils' writing was helping them to reinterpret the world about them, was valid. Writing *can* be valuable in that way: perhaps that is why I have written this document. But when our pupils wrote stories that reflected images from television and the novels they were reading, and when they wrote about what they presented as first-hand experience, were they always grappling with the meaning of the world? It would be possible to believe that what they were often grappling with were the expectations of their teachers, and the refusal of words to obey their commands. The approach I adopted was successful in that all pupils became more inventive in their uses of language, and – as I have shown – some became highly skilled. I still value what literature offers – to *some* pupils – but I think that we exaggerated its efficacy as a means of social and moral education.

At times the morality that we leant towards was too restricted: it focused upon interpersonal sensitivities and undervalued wider responsibilities. We took too little notice of how much writing in adult life is actively engaged with the world about us, responding, persuading, acknowledging, arguing and celebrating. I am sure that we were right when we made hesitant steps towards linking English with reading, writing and talking in the world outside school. Even for English teachers, writing is seldom an activity pursued for its own sake, as in writing poetry for one's own eyes alone. Adult writing of all kinds is normally embedded in a context of purposes; it is a kind of action upon the world through other people. It is not easy for schools, since they are organised to be at arms length from many of the more destructive forces in the world outside, to see to it that school activities become actions that influence students' lives – except in the trivial sense that they influence the grades they receive and the approval and disapproval of teachers. It is not the business of secondary schools directly to prepare their students for employment, of course; what I have in mind is that schools should devise ways of ensuring that their pupils experience an array of uses of speech and writing that approximate to those we need to use in order to take a full part in adult life.

The Classroom Conversation

When we invented the phrase "the classroom conversation" we were not merely acknowledging that our responsibilities included giving some attention to spoken language but making early steps towards recognising the role played by language in all learning, not just in English lessons. I am not referring to language as system – to grammar and semantics and so on – but to the effect of talking and writing upon how we think. When we put our thoughts and feelings into words we are making them more real to ourselves. Indeed, much of what we say or write hardly exists except as vague intentions until we *put it into words*. The importance of making our thoughts and feeling *real to ourselves* is that we thereby make them open to reflection, and therefore to evaluation and revision. This could hardly be more important for all of us:

developing the ability to take responsibility for our thinking and feeling is essential to becoming moral and social beings in our kind of society.

This talking and writing does not take place in a vacuum, however. Whenever we write or talk we do so in a context provided by not only by our culture as a whole but by the various groups to which we belong and the various modes of understanding provided by our educational and other experiences. This context is not static, however, but changing, continuously reinterpreted by all those about us whom we interact with and whose written words we read. We are never alone; whatever we write or say comes as a kind of *reply* to what has has been said and written before. When we talk together we are not only finding out what each of us means but we are creating a joint meaning, modifying the streams of meaning that constitute our lives, so that we continuously recreate ourselves and our world by living together and communicating. The idea of a classroom conversation in 1966 encapsulated for me an emerging understanding of how learning goes on and the importance to it of sharing meanings with others who can modify or validate them, and acknowledged the flowing and intangible quality of much of the understanding that we live by. But I could not have written these two paragraphs to explain its importance.

SIXTH FORM LITERATURE TEACHING

In discussing my teaching at Minchenden I said that in literature my emphasis fell upon what the students could do and understand, as against the transmission of values and skills, and that I tried to hand over to them as much as possible the task of interpreting the works of literature we were studying. This contrasts sharply with the more directive teaching of literature in the sixth form at Ruabon and with the values implicit in that approach. I ask myself how I feel now about the sets of questions about a novel through which I transmitted my own kind of *reading* at Ruabon, and the group investigations which I used in the Minchenden sixth form? Both were successful in their own terms, but I suspect that they offered advantages to different pupils, the latter being more appropriate to students who already had access to the attitudes and preferences of literary culture. At Minchenden the culmination of sixth form work on a novel or play was to identify themes and issues and to ask a group of students to take responsibility for investigating one of them, in order eventually to report back to the class. I encouraged the students to read a good deal more widely than the list of examination set books required, and asked them to write regularly about novels of their own choice, for I was more concerned that they develop responses of their own that they could substantiate than to insist that everything they wrote about was an important work of literature. Here too I was trying to move from the transmission of a standard view of literature towards encouraging the students to develop their own ability to read critically. At the same time I aimed to stress the relevance of literature to life by encouraging them to make choices.

Many of the sixth form students blossomed under this treatment, but there were others for whom it did not provide the amount of guidance that they wanted. One sixth form girl let me know via a teacher in another department that she would have preferred far more directed teaching. She had not been a strong member of the group, and had never seemed very interested in literature. However, as was perfectly proper, she needed a good examination grade for career purposes. In the event she passed the A-level examination in English Literature, but she believed that I could have helped her to a higher grade, and I think that would indeed have been the case if I had used the methods I had used at Ruabon. It is not easy to determine where the emphasis should fall in this clash of two principles. Today I don't know where I stand on this, though it was the open-ended approach – giving validity to the students' own constructions of the literary work – that led to my successful publications once I had moved into university work. I have no doubt that many of my students at Ruabon gained greatly from having detailed access to my way of interpreting a novel. They had no need to accept my view of *Emma* or *Passage to India* once the examination was past, and so far as general education is concerned I had given them a scaffolding that could guide their reading of any novel. On the other hand, it seems to me that in all parts of the curriculum – perhaps because of the nature of examinations – schools place too much emphasis upon the presentation of bodies of knowledge, so that students are discouraged from developing their ability to make sense of the world for themselves. The examination system however makes this almost inevitable, and it is far worse in some other countries, as *The Diploma Disease* made clear.

THE TEACHER'S RESPONSIBILITY

Through our emphasis upon *personal writing* and the students' choices of topic, and upon developing their own responses to works of literature, we were assigning considerable validity to their view of the world even when it conflicted with ours. How did teachers reconcile "having something to teach" with the validity we acknowledged in the learner's experience? How could we set and mark examinations on such terms? I was once charged by a group of teachers on an advanced course with having abandoned my values when I gave their essays a range of grades. They had interpreted my belief that learners should be given opportunities to interpret aspects of the world for themselves as equivalent to saying that a teacher should abandon his or her values. I was certainly not intending to say that "Anything Goes". My view is that responsible teachers do not go beyond the following.

- They realise that, since students' perspectives have validity for them, teachers need to understand what they are and take them into account.

- They delay overt judgement of students' contributions to lessons in order to give them opportunity to modify their own thinking.

- They provide opportunities for individual and group work.

- They discuss purposes and methods with students, and whenever possible negotiate them.

Since any new learning is built upon a reshaping of old understandings, it is never wise for teachers to ignore what their pupils already believe. Getting them to make their thinking explicit is often a first step to critical reflection upon the limitations of an existing perspective. Assigning temporary validity to students' current ideas for the purpose of classroom work, however immature those ideas may be, is not necessarily the same as abandoning values.

During the optimistic sixties it was all too easy for teachers to behave as if knowledge was somewhere *out there* for the students to stumble upon; *discovery learning* was a fashionable phrase. But we cannot just leave young people to their own devices as if all culture were there for the finding. It is a teacher's duty to help young people make sense of the world about them and this must include offering them cultural and intellectual tools for the purpose, but it is the learner who has to learn how to make use of these tools, and no teacher, however helpful, can do this for his or her pupils. Even when I was making much use of small group discussion, I do not think that I ever fell into the empiricist trap, as if the "buzzing, blooming" world about us had its meaning written across its face, so our pupils would only have to look in order to understand. I read Bruner's *The Process of Education* in 1964 – it had been recommended by Peter Doughty when he was a member of the LATE poetry working party – and it persuaded me that it was the teacher's job in all subjects of the curriculum to offer students an induction into ways of understanding, appreciating and acting already existing in the culture, in order to provide frames of reference for making sense of the world. (Similar assumptions were of course implicit in the Cambridge view of the teaching of literature.) At that time we had hardly begun to grasp the idea that culture is continuously remade in the course of living by ourselves, by our pupils, by all the people about us. (Nowadays, with the work of Bakhtin available, we have less excuse for being unaware.) This makes it all the more important to help young people to become reflective members of society.

After a lecture a science teacher once asked me to expound the reasons why I was recommending that more responsibility should be handed to the learners to explore their understanding through talk. Did I believe that it would improve their learning of science or did I think it was important for their social development, because it would help them to be critical and self-reliant learners in the future? It was indeed an acute question, which made me think hard then and afterwards. I do believe that an important part of teaching is to create occasions when every learner has to grapple for himself or herself with the problems of adapting new knowledge to existing understandings and strategies, though I acknowledge that some (but not by any means all) pupils achieve this through reading and written work. I also believe that schooling too often places learners in passive roles that send unhelpful messages about how one should approach new ideas and experiences, that is, about what constitutes good learning. It is now clear to me that both goals are important, though at times one or other of them was dominant in my thinking.

Teachers have sometimes interpreted what I later wrote as if I were recommending *laissez faire* in the classroom. I hope that I have made it clear in this account that I regarded small group methods as merely one option from a repertoire of ways of working, and that I was always quick to abandon the group format when my pupils were not working seriously. A teacher can present new material to a class and indicate a way of understanding it, but it is for the pupils to carry out the mental processes that lead to "understanding". They must work out how a new way of thinking presented by a teacher can be used to account for how things are, what are the limitations that should qualify its relevance, and how it can be turned into action. Having provided a frame of reference the teacher has the responsibility to set up opportunities for pupils to learn its uses and limitations, and this is where independent and group work came in. For this reason, I believed – and still believe – that it is important for students to have opportunities to explore through talk and writing their current understanding of the topic in hand, since that is the basis for any new learning, and even more important, that they should take active responsibility for their learning, so far as this can be achieved.

Recently my generation of English teachers has been criticised for having relied too much upon faith and assertion instead of carrying out a clear analysis of aims and methods. The criticism may have some validity. Phrases such as *personal development* and *response* were vague, though I have tried to show that they were more than mere slogans by explaining the ideas that underlay them. The kind of teaching that I have described in this book has had a bad press in recent years, and this is not only the result of political pressures from those who are suspicious of any attempts to encourage boys and girls to think for themselves. During those years our presentation of principles even to one another tended often to be vague, and I wonder whether their instability in classroom practice was partly the result of our failure to explain ourselves. Could they have been made more explicit without misrepresentation? One of the difficulties is that much of the content of the English curriculum as we then conceived of it was indeed intangible: do we want to omit from the curriculum our (perhaps high-flown) intention to influence our pupils' ethical sensibilities? Perhaps we were aiming at goals beyond our reach. Moreover, there was a serious lack of consensus amongst English teachers, which would have made such an analysis likely to be rejected or ignored. Teachers are faced daily with an immediate need to act in a classroom milieu that is extremely complex and with an awareness of conflicting demands coming from management, parents, colleagues, politicians and the pupils themselves. It is not surprising that many are impatient of analyses and make ad hoc choices of strategies that seem to "*work*".

STUDYING LANGUAGE

There is much confusion in people's understanding of the study of language. I can distinguish three meanings in current use of the word "grammar". It is used popularly to refer to conformity to received usage in any particular context, which we all value, and none more than English teachers. It is also used by academics to refer to systematic descriptions of language structures within the sentence, including the traditional system developed in earlier centuries to describe the Latin language and the many modern alternatives, such as the *transformational grammar* developed by Chomsky and others. However, it is not widely understood that when we speak and write we seldom consciously refer to such descriptions, and this is true even of professional grammarians who have spent their lives studying these systems. In practice, we generate language from an extremely complex set of systems that mainly work below the level of conscious thought. The third use of the word "grammar" refers to these systems and their output. Unfortunately it is far from obvious that learning about the second kind of grammar – one of the explicit descriptive systems, that is – will help students with the first kind of grammar – conforming to standard usage – or introduce changes in their ability to write and speak in a skilful and inventive way – which is part of the third meaning of "grammar". It is this confusion that makes the public discussion about the teaching of language so unhelpful. It is perfectly possible to teach the second kind of grammar to intelligent pupils – I did so during the early years of my teaching – but my colleagues and I abandoned it because we were far from convinced that our pupils were gaining from it. English teachers *do* value grammar in the first sense, but are not convinced that studying grammar in the second sense helps. We are left with questions. What kinds of study of language are *likely to influence young people's uses of language*? What will help them to write better prose? What will help them to understand what teachers tell them about inappropriate or incorrect usage? These are questions that have never been satisfactorily answered. I believe that some kinds of study of language are valuable, but I still do not believe that devoting many school hours to the systematic learning of a descriptive system (*grammar* number two), whether *traditional* or new, is likely to help, though there may be parts of the systems that it would be useful for students to understand. There seems to me to be every reason for the financing of a detailed research study of this issue, though I suspect that absolute certainty on this topic will never be achieved. There have been two earlier attempts: Michael Halliday's project in the seventies (which I have mentioned in earlier sections) published a handbook called *Language in Use,* which never had the notice that it deserved. More recently, the Conservative government set up the LINC project (Language in the National Curriculum) which produced extensive materials and advice to teachers, but these were not published by the government, presumably because they did not match their political dogmas about the teaching of language. Unfortunately the discussion of this important matter has too long been obscured by such rigid preconceptions.

IMPROVISED DRAMA

My attitude to the use of improvised drama has changed greatly during the last thirty years. I began using improvised drama in lessons more because I had been told it was important than on the basis of a properly thought out policy. The pupils enjoyed the lessons, and I began to experience the positive feelings that come from exercising expertise. It was not until some years later, after moving to university teaching, that I came seriously to question its value. One experienced teacher of English, much committed to improvisation methods, decided while following a course with me to investigate the effect of improvisation upon his pupils' language and understanding by tape-recording a series of attempts by the same groups of students to improvise a scene. Instead of an increase in the explicitness and complexity of the talk, as we both expected, these qualities seemed to decrease. It seemed that the more they practised the scene the more they were relying upon taken-for-granted knowledge of one another's meaning. I was perhaps too much influenced by this result, but it triggered scepticism of what I had formerly believed. If I were to teach English now I would give time to drama only for two purposes. It is the most appropriate way of entering a dramatic text. And it is a useful first approach through which students can explore their own and one another's attitudes to a value-laden topic, that is, it can be a powerful alternative to discussion.

THE INFLUENCE OF PUPILS

My teaching methods at Minchenden were undoubtedly influenced by the background of my pupils. A large proportion of them came from prosperous middle class homes, whose culture supported the school and its values, so that the boys and girls came to school with a tacit understanding of what was required, and a predisposition to please. Some came from homes where learning and intellectual and literary interests were highly valued, and the active interest of such pupils in our work together became an important dynamic that shaped my approach at the same time as my teaching shaped theirs. That is not to say, of course, that they were no times when individual young people or even groups were uncooperative. The kind of student-based work that I favoured there, with much collaboration in small groups, entirely depends for its success upon the students' willingness to accept the goals that the teacher has set. Without acceptance such an approach will fail, and directive teaching is more likely to succeed. Does this mean that student-based work always fails with groups of students who do not share the cultural advantages of my pupils at Minchenden? I think not. Indeed, when pupils do not immediately share the school's purposes there is much to be said for trying to negotiate goals that they can take seriously, though this is clearly more difficult in some other subjects than it is in English. I am sure that if I had been teaching in a comprehensive school both my manner and my subject matter would have had to be different, and perhaps I would not have been able to use exactly the methods I have described with all my classes. Pupils bring to lessons the frustration and indignation that have been generated elsewhere, in the school or outside, and this too plays a part in whether they will accept a teacher's goals for a lesson. My teaching would have been different in a different school, but it would have still been designed to show awareness of the pupils' perspectives and to encourage them to take responsibility for their own learning.

THINKING FOR THEMSELVES

I said in the *Introduction* that, though the sixties have been represented as a period of unrestrained self-indulgence, this did not apply to what my peers and I were attempting to do in English teaching. I believe that the English I taught was very disciplined, though I do accept that the values of that discipline were often implicit. Indeed, the very able fifth year girl who told me how much she had disliked writing in spite of the excellent work she had done had clearly found the implicit discipline so demanding as to spoil her enjoyment. I feel considerable indignation when the kind of teaching that I practised is called "trendy", for the teachers and lecturers who were members of LATE did not adopt it in pursuit of a fashion. Indeed, when I began to teach at Minchenden it was not *in fashion* since very few teachers were teaching in that way. I hope that I have been able in this account to make clear what principles guided our choices of teaching methods, which were never rigid or directed by dogmatism. I believe that if this country is to be an effective democracy, young people need not only to take over the competences that our culture offers but also to be able to think for themselves. Both are responsibilities of schooling.

13 Conditions for Change

When I first embarked upon this account of my teaching my purposes were simply autobiographical, to record an important part of my life, but as I wrote the task changed. It became more and more necessary to reflect upon the meaning of the experiences, and to see what happened from a wider perspective, which implied considering the contexts in which the changes took place. In this last section I take a further step back from the experiences, to see what generalisations might be drawn. Of course, in some respects my experiences were not representative, but I have tried in the previous pages to characterise them.

I want to consider what conditions are likely support teachers in attempting to improve their teaching, and what conditions hinder this. Their first need is to look critically at what happens in lessons, to try alternatives, and to evaluate the results. What will support them through the inevitable uncertainties and mistakes? What is likely to encourage the kind of reflection that leads to creative thinking about teaching? What will help them to distinguish the signs of emerging success, and leave behind unproductive ways of thinking and acting? In this section I summarise what I discovered in the course of writing this autobiographical essay about the conditions under which my own teaching changed during those years.

A crucial change that has occurred since that time is the arrival of the National Curriculum. During my years of teaching, we certainly did not feel completely free, for our work was constrained by examination requirements, parents' expectations, and powerful professional norms that were at times more cloying than encouraging of innovation. Nevertheless, the responsibility for the curriculum lay with the schools, and those of us who – perhaps with the support of organisations such as LATE – knew what direction we wanted to move in were free to try new methods, and to some extent new content. Most notably, I suppose, this was true in English. Even though some teachers have seemed to welcome the security provided by an official curriculum, I cannot but suspect that it inhibits the kind of innovation that we found so exciting, perhaps most by making teachers feel that their contributions are not valued.

THE SOURCES OF VALUES

I have frequently acknowledged in the course of this account the way in which the thinking of other people has influenced me, especially the Cambridge values of F.R. Leavis. As the years passed, the thinking of LATE and especially of James Britton took their place, with the additional force that came from providing a forum where teaching could be discussed with others. In the background were, of course, the values that I myself brought to the profession, these being powerfully influenced by my father, a lifelong socialist and member of the Labour Party. I also mentioned my own schooling, which though very mixed did include opportunities to sample what can be gained from liberal teaching methods. It must have been this background that made me so ready to take over the values of LATE and to develop some of the practical implications of those values.

My wife too was an English teacher. Throughout those years we talked over our work at great length, and undoubtedly influenced one another, but our conversations were so fully woven into the texture of my life that I find it impossible to separate them.

However, it is possible to overemphasise the influence of individual persons and of events, for the diverse messages that come from the institutional and cultural milieux in which teachers work are at least as powerful.

THE LONDON ASSOCIATION FOR THE TEACHING OF ENGLISH

It will be patent to the reader that LATE contributed enormously to my development as a teacher. With LATE should be bracketed the University of London Institute of Education, since many of the most significant figures in LATE were lecturers at the Institute. However, it was not just the Association's outstanding theorists that were important to my efforts to become a better teacher. A teacher's association which, unlike a union, is solely devoted to the pursuit of better education for pupils, provides an alternative milieu for the development and cherishing of new procedures and the values that underlie them. When the values of a particular school are less sympathetic, the presence of an outside source of values can be very important, as I had found at Dartford and Ruabon. Evening lectures that provided new ideas for lessons were helpful in my earlier days in the Association, but later I was more influenced by carefully planned week-end conferences, and perhaps most of all by the working parties that I took part in, especially those on the examining of literature, on short stories and on the teaching of poetry. It was the LATE conferences and working parties that provided detailed enough discussion to open up radically different ways of understanding the teaching of English. It seems a pity that all teachers cannot benefit from such opportunities.

An incidental influence that came as a by-product of my participation in LATE and in other activities at the Institute of Education was the increased visibility of my teaching, and wider access to audiences for my ideas. That visitors were interested to observe and discuss my teaching, and that I was invited to speak and write articles about it, inevitably encouraged me to take it more seriously.

BOOKS AND ARTICLES

Books and articles on educational topics played remarkably little part in my thinking right up to the last two or three years of teaching, when I became aware of the work of Bruner and Vygotsky on language and learning. For many years my wife and I read the journal *Use of English* to which I myself contributed. This will certainly have tended to reinforce the values I learnt at Cambridge, but when I looked back through the articles I must have read during those years I could not find a single one that had undoubtedly changed my teaching. Books on drama provided activities for improvisation, and *The Excitement of Writing* reinforced ideas about helping pupils to explore experience. Some textbooks may have played a part in the earliest years, including *Reading and Discrimination* for sixth form teaching and an unusual anthology of poetry, *The Poet's Tongue*. But naming these is misleading since their roles were at most peripheral. My main reading continued to be in English literature. The idea of writing as an exploration of everyday life was given support by the novels and verse of the period, while the shadow of D.H. Lawrence's writings about family and other relationships fell across most English teachers at that time.

THE COMMUNITY

It would be too easy solely to identify influential ideas and the persons from whom they came and to ignore the crucial force of the values current in the wider community and in the particular schools I taught in. As we moved from the nineteen fifties into the sixties, the national ethos became more optimistic and more liberal; collaboration became more highly valued and the effect of competition upon the fortunes of the losers became a matter of concern. There was an increasing sense that education was failing a large part of the community, and this was thought to arise not only from economic and social disadvantage but also because cultural differences led some teachers to devalue the abilities that learners already had. Writers celebrated working class culture. Sensitivity to our students and to what they brought to lessons became highly valued. Without this background of values outside in the community it would have been difficult to carry out the liberalising changes that many contemporary English teachers were engaged in. One source of influence was the BBC, which tried to combine popularity with high cultural and intellectual standards, for *pop culture* had not then taken over the media so powerfully as it later did.

SCHOOLS, HEADMASTERS AND COLLEAGUES

The characteristics of the schools as institutions had a marked effect on my teaching. I am very conscious of the difference between the ambitious instrumentality of the Dartford school in the mid fifties and the liberalism of Minchenden School in the early sixties, with a sympathetic headmaster, himself a literary critic, who supported my innovations. In other respects too the four schools I taught in were very different, for in every school pupils transmit strong implicit messages, partly their own and partly from their parents, about what they are willing to value. Teachers are more influenced by their pupils than they sometimes admit, for without the pupils' collaboration little will be learnt, however hard the teacher labours. This influence was of course oblique, being expressed by the themes which pupils accepted most enthusiastically, the issues they themselves introduced, and the activities that produced the best work. The professional class families of the Minchenden area supported a school ethos that was sympathetic to liberal teaching methods so long as examination results remained good.

I must emphasis too the great importance to me of my colleagues in the English department at Minchenden, who were extremely supportive. I can hardly exaggerate how much I owe to them, and to several teachers of other subjects, who shared successes and failures with us over a cup of coffee in the staffroom. In previous schools it would have been perceived as inappropriate to discuss failures or even successes; teachers talked about pupils but not about teaching. At Minchenden we were able to offer suggestions to one another, and to propose rationales that spread across subjects and different curricula; it was a great support to share experiences in this way.

EXAMINATIONS

It was impossible to ignore examinations and the models of English that were inherent in them, so that the early activities in LATE to plan and put into effect alternative examinations were essential. However, as the demands of the General Certificate in Education changed, partly in response to our efforts, we found ourselves with considerable freedom to teach in the ways that we had come to value. Moreover, by the mid sixties many of us were members of committees that were charged with the planning of a new examination, the Certificate of Secondary Education, that was to be suitable for a larger proportion of the population, those who had been excluded by the GCE. I left the classroom too early to prepare pupils for the new examination, but taking part in the planning was an incentive to think more deeply about the curriculum and its testing.

NEW TECHNOLOGY

Although I suspect that a culture usually generates and adapts new technologies to its emerging purposes, I have no doubt that in the case of *the tape recorder* the new technology changed my values, not by making new methods available but by supporting reflection. As I have explained, the possibility of listening at leisure to my pupils discussing topics I had given them changed radically my view of the range and usefulness of small group talk. I don't think that the arrival of other technologies made any difference to my teaching.

PARTICULAR OCCASIONS

Although when I undertook this account of my teaching I thought that I would be identifying many occasions and events that made for change, I have hardly been able to do so, and there seems little point in rehearsing the one or two that I have already described. Change in teaching methods is seldom a matter of a sudden flash of insight, but rather an interaction between methods and perspectives, each influencing the other. Donald Schön's distinction between *espoused values* and *values in action* goes far to explain this. In a skilled activity like teaching, the values shown in our actions are often out of step with those we have consciously espoused. In order to bring them into line, our values in action must become conscious and this is achieved by reflecting upon what we do, and by trying alternatives and observing the results. When a teacher tries to change his or her teaching simply by following a recipe this frequently is unsuccessful because, unknown to the teacher, the unconscious *values in action* take over. Equally, the traditional method of improving teaching by changing teachers' espoused values all too frequently becomes mere lip-service to the new values. Change depends upon both conscious and unconscious patterns of understanding and action, and requires a process of interaction between them that may be lengthy but cannot be omitted. There were one or two critical moments in my development as a teacher – one being the occasion when Harold Rosen brought a group of students to my lesson – but their function was to bring into focus changes that were already partly taking place.

FINDING SOLUTIONS

In rereading what I have written in earlier sections I have come to realise that some of the more inventive teaching came as solutions to problems in achieving goals that I had accepted. For example, it was when I realised that my teaching of writing about less personal topics was ineffective that I began to discover ways of *modelling* at the blackboard the processes of planning. The questions about novels that I gave to the sixth form at Ruabon were developed in order to help them to read more perceptively. It was in order to persuade pupils to write about their first-hand experiences in an expressive, lively and honest way that I began to find ways of using poems, improvised drama, and different kinds of class discussion to help them see what was required and give them confidence in their ability to supply it. One of the reasons for embarking upon group work was that it offered a partial solution to the problems of involving all of the pupils in a class in discussion, after I had seen that some played too passive a role in lessons. But I would not have perceived these as problems in need of solution without sets of values that were certainly not of my own creation.

IN CONCLUSION

We all want teachers to be more successful. I hope that I have persuaded the reader that changing how a teacher teaches is not a simple matter, to be achieved by a quick course on recommended procedures or by urging him or her to work harder. The contexts in which teachers work, both outside and inside the school, are crucial both in enabling him or her to perceive alternatives, and in supporting the process of change. So are the relationships between teachers in the same school. Theory and practice must develop hand-in-hand, and that takes time and the support of colleagues and superiors. I found that having a source of values outside the school, as well as inside it, was important, but I don't know how general that is. I found that I was more willing to take the risk of making changes when my morale was high, which makes me think that the destructive criticism of schools that has been characteristic of the last two decades is not likely to have helped teachers to improve.